AFRICAN COO

AFRICAN COOKERY BOOK

MARY OMINDE

HEINEMANN KENYA
NAIROBI

Published by
Heinemann Kenya Ltd.,
P.O. Box 45314, Kijabe Street, Nairobi.

LONDON IBADAN SINGAPORE KUALA LUMPUR
NEW DELHI AUCKLAND MELBOURNE SYDNEY

© Mary Ominde 1975
First published 1975
Reprinted 1984
Reprinted 1988

Text illustrations and
cover design by David Carnegie

ISBN 9966 46 480 8

Printed by Kenya Litho Ltd.,
P.O. Box 40775, Changamwe Road, Nairobi.

CONTENTS

INTRODUCTION iii

PART ONE
Kitchen and Store 1
Nutrition and Diets 4
Marketing and Storing food 10
Cooking and Hygiene 12

PART TWO
Weights and Measures 17
Glossary of terms used in the Recipes 17

AFRICAN RECIPES

Meat 22
Chicken 26
Fish 28
Groundnut 32
Maize & Maizemeal 36
Sweet Potato 52
Cassava 57
Matoke 62
Coconut 66
Mixtures 71
Special 81

ASIAN RECIPES 86

EUROPEAN RECIPES

Appetizers 94
Soups 96
Main Dishes 99
Stuffings 117
Dishes from Leftovers 120
Puddings 126

GENERAL

Eggs	132
Bread	135
Cakes	138
Biscuits	141
Dishes for Invalids	143

PART THREE

Home Remedies and Household Hints	147
Index	151

INTRODUCTION

This book is written for the younger generation of new housewives who may be interested in improving family cooking and are in need of guidance wherever they may be.

The book attempts to remind the housewives of the importance of a balanced diet when planning the family menu, especially where there are children. This in itself is a contribution to the development of nation building, as it is one way of fighting diseases. In the book, special consideration for individual members of the family is taken into account, starting from infants, children, adolescents, adults doing special jobs, expectant and nursing mothers, invalids up to the elderly.

Secondly the recipes selected are intended to suit every budget. These include some inexpensive balanced diets which homes with less income can afford to buy such as irio, green vegetable served as main dish with ugali and cooked in milk, or ebinyebwa served with matoke or lumonde. On the other hand the book also includes some recipes for special occasions which require more money such as stuffed mutura, chicken tandoori, barbecue pork chops or roast turkey.

Thirdly, methods of cooking mentioned in the book are intended for housewives living in towns as well as for those living in rural areas. Town dwellers can afford to own modern cookers and use electricity or gas. These housewives could do baking and oven roasting as well as all other methods of cooking mentioned in the book. With the steaming method, they could use aluminium foil or greaseproof paper for food wrapping. Housewives living in the rural areas on the other hand may not be able to make use of modern cookers but they can use pot roasting method or barbecue as well as using all other cooking methods apart from baking. Banana leaves could be used when steaming food as opposed to aluminium foil or greaseproof paper which their counterparts in the towns may use.

Fourthly, the housewife's job has been made easier in this book by using utensils available in all houses, when dealing with weights and measures. The measuring of weights and volumes either in the Standard or Metric system will not be a problem, wherever the housewife may be.

Dishes included in the book represent a cross section of the community in this part of the world. Ugandan dishes are ebinyebwa, matoke and lumonde, coconut milk dishes with rice or ugali are from Tanzania and irio, mutura and ugali are some of the Kenyan dishes.

European and Asian dishes are included in the book mainly because there are many Asians and Europeans whose home is in East Africa, and also because many of these recipes are of local foodstuffs. Moreover these are new dishes which will add variety to the menu already known by the younger generation of new housewives.

Traditionally soup and puddings or sweets are not served with African dishes. In the book, a few of these dishes are included to give the housewife a wider choice of a balanced diet when preparing the family menu, especially milk pudding and nourishing soup when catering for children and invalids.

Some remedies and household hints are included at the end of this book in the belief that any housewife using the book may find them useful. Home remedies may help as emergency measures in places where the family lives far from health clinics.

At first this book was meant to be translated into Swahili to be used as a sister to the Kenya Cookery Book. For this reason some of the dishes and explanations are extremely simple. It was later decided that more housewives would benefit from the book if published in English.

Mary Ominde.

Part 1

KITCHEN AND STORE

PLANNING

The design of a kitchen should be on a labour-saving basis so that it is more economic to run and a joy in which to work.

It is important that forward progressive movement from store to dining-room is established so that paths do not cross.

Cookery smells should be prevented from spreading through the house by an arrangement of walls or partitions.

POSITION

The kitchen should be at the rear of the house on the ground floor. If it is attached to the house it should have back door access to avoid passing through the main house.

It should be near the dining-room to avoid walking when serving meals.

Avoid a position near a source of dirt and noise such as near a busy road.

SIZE

Consideration should be given to the number of people to be catered for, the type of meals and fuel used.

A kitchen should be large enough to provide comfortable working space.

There should be adequate storage space.

VENTILATION AND LIGHTING

Good ventilation is essential both for health and for the comfort of the housewife.

Good lighting is also essential. Place lanterns above eye level on a stand.

One good sized window should suffice for both ventilation and light.

FLOOR AND WALLS
Use a surface flooring which can be cleaned easily.

Use surface materials for the walls which are white in colour and easily cleaned.

THE STORE OR LARDER
The store should have good light, ventilation, absolute cleanliness, adequate space, coolness, dryness and should be constructed of materials which can easily be cleaned.

KITCHEN FITTINGS
1. Cooking Stoves
Wood or charcoal cooking stoves are very useful as they hold the ashes and the fire is not in direct contact with the floor.

Modern stoves are locally available but are costly. Such stoves are designed for use with charcoal, oil, gas and electricity. Gas stoves are becoming more and more popular as the availability of gas supplies spreads throughout the country.

Oven Temperature

Different makes of cookers may vary and even the same makes of cookers could give slightly different results at the same temperature. The following are only approximate guides which are quite a good average in every case. (Refer to your own manufacturer's temperature chart when there is doubt).

OVEN CHART FOR BAKING
(The centre of the oven only)

DESCRIPTION OF OVEN	ELECTRIC °F	GAS Thermostat setting
1. Very cool	200–250	$\frac{1}{4}$–$\frac{1}{2}$
2. Slow or cool	250–300	1–2
3. Very moderate	300–350	2–4
4. Moderate	350–375	4–5
5. Moderately hot to hot	375–400	5–6
6. Hot to very hot	400–500	6–8

Simple test for oven temperature
1. Heat the oven until the food is ready to go in (approximately 10–15 minutes).

2. Place a plain white piece of paper in the centre of the oven and leave for 3 minutes. The colour of the piece of paper shows the oven temperature.
   (a) black: the oven is far too hot.
   (b) deep brown: the oven is very hot.
   (c) golden brown: the oven is hot.
   (d) light brown: the oven is moderately hot.
   (e) biscuit colour: the oven is slow or cool.

Make sure that the oven temperature is correct before putting the food inside.

2. Furniture

It is very important to have a few essential pieces of furniture for use in the kitchen.

Table: Choose a strong table which is easy to keep clean. A table with a formica top is ideal.

Cupboard: It should be strong and easy to keep clean.

Meat Safe: This is very essential for keeping flies away from food and safeguarding the health of the family.

Stool: A few stools should be placed in the kitchen for use by the housewife and her friends.

Basin: Wash hand basin or water jug: Towel: Soap. These are very essential for personal hygiene. Housewives must always wash their hands before and after touching food.

3. Utensils

Cooking utensils should be of good quality and in adequate supply. It is impossible to cook good meals when cooking implements are poor and insufficient. The following are some of the essential requirements but the choice should be related to the type of cooker used.

Pots and Pans: Three or four good quality heavy aluminium pans are suitable depending of course on the size of the family.

Spoons: Select different sizes and types. Metal spoons of various sizes should be used for different courses as well as for handy measures. Wooden spoons are used for stirring food when being cooked.

Knives: Select different sizes and include some for cutting meat, chopping and slicing vegetables and slicing bread, as well as those used at table for different courses.

Plates and Bowls: Strong plates or bowls of different sizes made from good quality enamel are very useful. These can be used for

food mixing or for serving.
The housewife should select all other utensils bearing in mind her method of cooking.

NUTRITION AND DIETS

Our bodies require a balanced diet every day so that we can enjoy good health. Good health means that our bodies can meet the following needs.

GROWTH

A newly-born baby is very small but it grows every day and eventually becomes an adult. If the same baby is denied good food its body fails to grow and the baby may die. From this we learn it is good food which makes a baby grow healthy and reaches adulthood.

REPAIR

The body of an adult is like a house which needs repair from time to time. Without proper food the body becomes wasted and eventually collapses. The types of food which make a baby grow and also repair the worn out parts of the body are called Protein foods. Protein is found in meat, poultry, fish, cheese, eggs, milk, beans, peas, nuts and unpolished cereals.

STRENGTH

After strenuous activity the body becomes exhausted. When tired, people sit down to rest and take some refreshment; in this way they get their strength back. But if they miss many meals, their bodies become weaker until they find it impossible to move because their strength is finished. From this we learn that food is the source of strength. Foods which supply the body with strength are called carbohydrates, and these are found in cereals, grain, sugar, potatoes, cassava, yams and arrow-root.

WARMTH

When the body is cold, we become warm again after doing physical activities. There must be a store from which we draw our warmth and this store is built by food consumed. Foods which provide warmth to the body are called fats and oils. Fat is found in butter, cream, ghee and animal fat. Oil is found in oily fish, nuts and certain vegetables from which vegetable oil is made.

PROTECTION AND MAINTENANCE

The body could easily absorb germs because of diseases or accidents. It is impossible to see these germs and yet a healthy body can escape some of them. Food protects the body from such germs and also maintains it in a healthy condition. Foods which provide protection and maintenance to the body are called vitamins and minerals and are found in fruits, vegetables, milk, butter, cheese, millet, simsim, common salt and meat.

CLEANLINESS

As we know it is impossible to wash the inner parts of the body. Food keeps the inside of the body clean by ridding it of unwanted matter. These foods are known as roughage.

WATER

Good health demands water. Water carries food value from the stomach to all parts of the body, it carries heat from food to all parts of the body, it is the foundation of the body's blood and it keeps the body clean.

Any meal which contains protein, carbohydrates, fat, oil, vitamins, minerals, is part of a Balanced Diet.

PLANNING A BALANCED DIET FOR A FAMILY

Children especially require a balanced diet every day. The following points should be considered when planning a family's menu.
- a. Satisfy hunger by giving ample carbohydrates.
- b. Supply sufficient proteins.
- c. Give plenty of vitamins and minerals.
- d. Ensure the family has sufficient roughage, drinks plenty of water daily.
- e. Supply sufficient fats and oils.

A SPECIMEN BALANCED DIET FOR CHILDREN FROM 1 TO 5 YEARS

	Breakfast	Lunch	Tea	Supper
SUNDAY	Fresh orange juice. Egg—scrambled or boiled. Buttered toast. Milk.	Roast young chicken. Chopped roast potatoes. Chopped green vegetables. Fruit salad and cream. Milk.	Maize flour doughnuts mixed with eggs. Passion fruit juice.	Fried fish. Potato chips. Green vegetables. Coconut sauce. Milky cocoa.
MONDAY	Fresh paw-paw. Maize flour porridge with milk and sugar	Fried liver. Mashed potatoes. Green vegetables. Fruit salad. Milk.	Buttered corn scones. Fresh pineapple juice.	Steamed sweet potatoes with groundnut sauce. Milk.
TUESDAY	Fresh orange. Whole wheat porridge with milk and sugar.	Stewed chicken. Steamed plantain. Green vegetables. Fruit salad. Milk.	Cake. Fresh tangerine juice.	Steamed fresh fish in cheese sauce. Mashed potatoes. Green vegetables. Milky cocoa.
WEDNESDAY	Fresh mango. Finger millet porridge with milk and sugar.	Stewed meat. Steamed plantain. Green vegetables. Fruit salad. Milk.	Wheat flour doughnuts mixed with eggs. Lemon juice.	Dried fish stewed with ugali and green vegetables. Milk.

THURSDAY	Pineapple. Sorghum flour porridge with milk and sugar.	Mince of lean mutton. Boiled rice. Green vegetables. Fruit salad. Milk.	Peanut butter sandwiches. Fresh orange juice.	Soft boiled beans. Fried sausages. Bread and butter. Milky cocoa.
FRIDAY	Fresh banana. Oatmeal porridge with milk and sugar.	Stewed fresh fish with Ugali. Green vegetables. Fruit salad. Milk.	Cakes. Mango juice.	Plantain in coconut milk. Boiled egg. Milk.
SATURDAY	Fresh tangerine. Finger millet flour porridge with milk and sugar.	Stewed beef. Boiled mashed potatoes. Fruit salad. Milk.	Maize flour biscuits, mixed with eggs and buttered. Passion fruit juice.	Groundnuts sauce. Poached egg. Steamed cassava. Milky cocoa.

Children should be given plenty of clean water to drink with each meal. Give them also something hard such as toast for biting on to strengthen their teeth. Fruit and vegetables mentioned above must be changed according to their availability in the season.

Considerations for individual members of the family

Special consideration should be given for members of the family who may need more of certain kinds of foods due to health or age.

Expectant mother

A woman who enjoys a good diet during pregnancy will usually give birth to a healthy and well-formed baby. She should eat plenty of protein for the baby's growth as well as for the maintenance of her own body. The expectant mother should also eat food which contains plenty of vitamins and minerals for protection against disease. She should continue to eat all other types of food normally taken by the other members of her family.

Nursing mother

Nursing mother's diet should be the same as that given above except that she requires larger amounts of protein, vitamins, minerals and liquids to produce the milk to feed the baby.

Infants

An infant can live very satisfactorily on its mother's milk for the first few months. If this is not available then the baby should be fed on cow's milk. If cow's milk is the infant's main food, the following foods could be added to it.
   a. Sugar and water.
   b. Orange juice or other fruit juice for vitamins as these are not contained in cow's milk.
   c. Egg and sieved green vegetables to give more vitamins when the baby is about 6 months old.

Children from 1-5 years—See the above chart, Page oo.

Children of primary school age

At this age children grow very fast and therefore have great need for proteins, vitamins and minerals. They are very active and therefore have a great need for carbohydrates. The food should not be too bulky because the stomach is small. Give plenty of milk, eggs, meat, cheese, fruits and vegetables.

Adolescents

Healthy adolescents have very big appetites because at this stage children are extremely active and are still growing. Give plenty of proteins, vitamins, minerals and carbohydrates. Their requirements are greater than those of adults engaged in similar activities.

Adult heavy worker
An adult doing heavy manual work requires energy both for the upkeep of his body and for physical work. His food should be rich in fats and oils. Give plenty of salt to replace the losses during perspiration.

Sedentary worker
An adult who performs light manual duties such as a clerk, typist or shop assistant, must have roughage foods increased. Give him more fruit and vegetable salads and food prepared with wholemeal flour.

Vegetarian
Some vegetarians eat cheese, milk, ghee and cream. If food is to be prepared for such a person in your household, give more of this type of food to provide protein. Also give pulses and beans and other vegetables. A strict vegetarian will only eat beans, pulses and nuts. In that case use extra amount of vegetable which can provide the necessary proteins and also vegetable oils in the diet to increase energy.

Middle-age
When an adult reaches middle-age he becomes less active. His diet therefore should contain less sugar, starch and fat.

Old age
In an old person the amount of food required decreases because his stomach becomes smaller and because he is less active. Give a well-balanced diet containing all essential food requirements. The food must be well-cooked, nourishing and easily digested. Remember that an old person's teeth are weak and cannot chew food properly. Give several small meals each day so that the stomach is not over-loaded. Avoid tough meat, raw vegetables and fried food. Give plenty of milk. The diet should include plenty of proteins, vitamins and calcium.

Invalids
Invalid diet consists of liquid, light and convalescent foods, but the type of food served depends on a particular illness.
Liquid: given to a person who is very ill and unable to eat. It can be roughly divided into three types of food: nutritive; e.g.

egg in milk, porridge and so on; refreshing, e.g. lemonade, and stimulant, e.g. beef, tea and soups, and so on.

Light: given to a patient who is beginning to recover from a serious illness. It includes all liquid diets plus minced chicken, beef, mutton, fish, eggs, egg and cheese dishes.

The doctor's advice should be strictly followed when giving invalid diets. (See invalid dishes on page 143-6).

MARKETING AND STORING FOOD

It pays to shop personally especially when buying fish and meat. Experience helps in choosing food.

MARKETING RULES

Make a list of things you require before shopping. Be economical and buy only what is really needed. Buy only non-perishable goods in bulk.

Be observant and compare prices from different shops or markets.

Buy where you know the food is usually fresh. Buy from a clean stall or shop which is free from flies. Always buy food in season. It is more fresh then, and cheaper.

Shop early in the day especially when purchasing fish, meat and green vegetables to ensure freshness.

Leave the buying of perishable foods, especially meat and fish until last so that you take home the food while it is still fresh.

Avoid false economies by buying cheap food which in the end has to be thrown away.

HINTS ON CHOICE OF FOOD

Meat

Meat should be elastic to the touch. It should have a pleasant smell. (If in doubt of freshness, insert a knife near the bone, remove it and then smell). It should be bright red, moist and with no discoloration. Inferior meat always appears dark.

Fat should be creamy in colour and evenly distributed.

Fish

Fish is at its best when it is in season. All fish must be absolutely fresh, especially the oily kinds.

It should have a pleasant smell and colour. The fish's eyes should be bright and prominent, not dull and sunken. The scales should be plentiful, bright and shiny. The tail should be straight, not drooping. The gills should be clear, bright and red, never brown. Flesh should be firm and elastic to touch. Avoid buying fish on Mondays as it may be Saturday's leftovers.

Dried Fish
The flesh should be firm, not soft. There should be no unpleasant smell. It should not be too dry. Make sure the fish is free from maggots.

Green vegetables
They should be bright green, fresh and attractive with no yellow tints. They should be firm to the touch with crisp leaves, not wilted nor broken. The leaves should be whole, not insect-eaten. Cabbages and lettuce should have close hearts. Cauliflowers should have close hearts with white centre.

Root vegetables
All root vegetables should be smooth, fresh and heavy. They should be of medium size, well-shaped and firm to the touch. They should be free from bruises, wrinkles and worms. Onions should be well-covered with natural skin.

Dried Beans and corn
These should be heavy and free from weevils, fresh-looking, not wilted. They should not contain any dirt and sand.

Corn on the cob
The corn should be firmly fixed on the cob. Corn should be fresh-looking and whole. Corn should be free from insects and their bites.

Fruit
Fruit should be fresh-looking and firm. It should be free from insect bites, mould and bruises.

Coconuts
The shell should look fresh and pale. There should be plenty of liquid inside when shaken. (If the liquid is dried up, the coconut is old). The coconut should have a clean, white flesh with no discoloration when opened. The white skin should be free from slime and smell.

STORING OF FOOD

Perishable foods (meat, fish, milk, etc.)
Buy in small quantities and store in a refrigerator or in a meat safe placed in a cool room. Cook such foods immediately unless you have a refrigerator with a deep-freeze compartment.

Vegetables and fruits
Store in a cool room away from light. Place in a basket or in a wire rack raised off the ground to allow good air circulation.

Flour
Store in a fine basket or bag raised off the ground and placed in a dry, cool place.

Beans and pulses and cereals
Shell and dry thoroughly and then sprinkle with chemical or ashes to preserve from weevils. Store in a basket or sack raised off the ground. Put out in the sun from time to time.

Sugar
Store in a bin placed in a dry room.

Tea and Coffee (also spices)
Store in an airtight tin.

Salt
Store in a bottle placed in a very dry place.

Preserved food
Store in a dark, cool and dry place (heat and dampness bring mould).

COOKING AND HYGIENE

REASONS FOR COOKING

Food is prepared and cooked for various reasons; to increase the food value, to improve the flavour, to facilitate digestion, to improve the appearance, to eliminate the risk of infection from harmful bacteria, and, to make chewing and swallowing easier.

FOOD CONTAMINATION

Public Health authorities are taking a keen interest in cleanliness of food offered for sale especially in towns. However, the possibility of the spread of diseases by food is still enormous.

Some diseases which are carried in and spread by food are: dysentery, tuberculosis, diptheria and diarrhoea, the first three often caused by germs carried in milk.

HYGIENE IN THE KITCHEN
General
Boil all milk and keep it in a meat-safe or refrigerator. Keep the store and kitchen free from flies, rats, cockroaches and other kitchen pests.
Wash all food utensils in hot water.
Collect kitchen refuse in a bin and burn it.
Scrub sinks with a branded kitchen cleaner.
Never prepare food on the ground where germs from dust and dirt could easily reach the food.
Make a habit of rinsing out pans that are not in daily use before using them.

Personal
Hygiene in the kitchen begins with the cook as many diseases can be spread when handling food. It is impossible for a dirty person to prepare clean meals. The cook should remember and practice the following rules:

She should see that her hands are scrubbed, nails cut and hair tidy and covered with a head cloth before cooking.

She should not put her fingers in her mouth, ears or nose while cooking or serving food.

She should always wash her hands after visiting the lavatory or touching personal parts of her body.

A handkerchief should always be used when the cook has a cold and it must be kept in her pocket.

All cuts should be covered with a sterilised waterproof dressing.

She must keep away from the kitchen if she is suffering from any infectious disease.

Any sign of any disease which are commonly spread by food should be reported immediately. The person concerned should stop handling food. A medical examination is very necessary and treatment given at once.

METHODS OF COOKING

BOILING

Boiling is cooking by total immersion in boiling water. It is a simple and popular method which is suitable for most foods. Cheaper cuts of meat can be cooked in this way. To achieve the best results, place the meat in a strong pan and use just sufficient water to cover the meat. Boil for 5 minutes, then reduce the heat. Keep the liquid simmering until the meat is soft. For vegetables, bring the water to the boil first, then add salt before putting in the vegetables. Keep the water boiling all the time until the vegetables are cooked. Fish and eggs should be boiled with the water just at boiling point. The time taken for fish varies according to weight, age of the fish and also the type.

STEWING

This method is used mainly for meat, poultry and fish. The food is cooked in a small amount of liquid, either water or stock, in a pot with a tight-fitting lid, using gentle heat over a long period. It is an economical way of cooking because cheaper cuts of meat can be used and very little fuel is consumed.

To achieve the best results: use a strong pan with a tight-fitting lid—earthen pots are the best. Cut the food into small pieces. Vegetables such as onions and carrots can also be added, chopped into small pieces. Keep the liquid simmering and make sure that there is enough liquid for gravy.

STEAMING

Steaming is cooking in steam rising from boiling water. The method often used in Africa is called the direct method.

Direct Method of Steaming

1. Place leaves from banana, millet or maize stalks in the bottom of a pot on crossed banana ribs.
2. Wrap the food in leaves from banana, millet or maize and place on the first layer of leaves in the pot.
3. Add sufficient water to touch the layer of leaves.
4. Place another layer of leaves over the food and cover the pot with a tight-fitting lid, sealed carefully with millet dough.
5. Cook until ready.

N.B. The modern method of steaming is to use a pressure cooker, or where only a normal saucepan is available, aluminium foil or greaseproof paper is used instead of banana leaves.

To achieve the best results: food should never touch the water; the water must be kept boiling all the time. If more water is needed during cooking, add only boiling water.

FRYING

Frying is cooking in hot fat or oil. There are two methods: shallow and deep frying.

Shallow Frying:
1. Take a shallow or flat-bottomed pan (*karai*) or a frying pan.
2. Pour in sufficient oil or fat to cover the bottom of the pan.
3. Heat the oil or fat and add the food.

Deep Frying:
1. Use a deep pan so that the hot fat is well below the top of the pan.
2. The fat or oil should be smoking hot before frying so that the food is sealed when added to the pan, otherwise the fat will get inside the food.
3. Fry a few pieces at a time otherwise the fat will cool down.
4. Fry the food to a regular golden brown colour.
5. Fried food should be carefully drained on absorbent paper, with the exception of meat.

ROASTING

Roasting is cooking by direct heat. Cooking in this way can be roughly divided into three groups: barbecue, pot and oven roasting.

Barbecue:
1. Place a metal grid over a charcoal fire which should have been burning for about half an hour.
2. Place the food on the grid.
3. Keep turning the food until cooked evenly on both sides.

Meat cooked in this way has an excellent flavour but tends to lose its juices. To achieve the best results: choose tender pieces of meat. Trim and season well before roasting. Avoid piercing the flesh as this will cause the juice to ooze out. Turn frequently to avoid burning.

Pot Roasting:
Pot roasting uses a pan with the heat underneath.
1. Use a strong pan and cook on a low heat.
2. Use a little oil in the pan to prevent sticking.
3. Place the meat in the hot oil.
4. Season well before cooking.
5. Turn the meat frequently at the beginning to seal it.
6. Cover with a tight-fitting lid and turn occasionally.

Oven Roasting:
This is a modern method which can only be done with modern stoves which have an oven. The food is cooked by the radiation of dry heat from all around it. Hot air in the oven is heated from the top, bottom and sides; the hot air cooks the food. This method is convenient and economical and for these reasons it has taken the place of other kinds of roasting.
1. Roast only tender meat and young birds.
2. A large piece of meat should be cooked because it will shrink during roasting.
3. Heat the oven for about 10-15 minutes before putting in the meat.
4. Place the meat on thick slices of potato or on a wire tray inside the pan to prevent the bottom from overcooking.
5. Expose the meat to a high temperature for the first 10-15 minutes to seal the surface, then reduce the heat and cook slowly until the meat is tender.
6. Pour hot oil or fat over the meat occasionally to prevent it drying up.

Part 2

WEIGHTS AND MEASURES

In this book, confusion is avoided by using the standard measuring breakfast cup*, dessert spoon and tea spoon.

The following are the detailed weights and measures (simplified to the nearest whole number) in case a check is required before cooking.

DRY MATERIALS:

Flour and similar light materials
- 1 cupful = 4 ozs. = 120 grams
- 4 cupfuls = 1 lb. = 480 grams
- 2 spoonfuls = 1 oz. = 30 grams

Sugar and similar heavy materials
- 1 cupful = 8 ozs. = 240 grams
- 2 cupfuls = 1 lb. = 480 grams
- 1 spoonful = 1 oz. = 30 grams

Icing sugar
- 1½ cupfuls = 8 ozs. = 240 grams

LIQUID MATERIALS:
- 2 cupfuls = 1 pint = 500 ml (millilitre)

BUTTER, MARGARINE AND FATS:
- 1 cupful = 8 ozs. = 240 grams
- 1 spoonful = 1 oz. = 30 grams

GLOSSARY OF COOKERY TERMS USED IN THE RECIPES

Almonds Seeds of a fruit in the plum family which could be used chopped or ground or even whole, in cakes and puddings.

Arrow-root Root of a tropical plant in the cassava family. It could be used in the same way as cassava.

Au-gratin Certain dishes mixed with white sauce, topped with crisp breadcrumbs and browned on top.

Bala (Sesquicarbonate) Luo word. A certain type of salt found particularly in Nyanza Province.

Batter A mixture of flour and liquid such as milk or water to which eggs are sometimes added.

Bay-leaf Leaf of a certain tree found in West Indies. The leaf is used in certain dishes for flavouring purposes.

Biltong S. African word. Cured and dried meat.

To blanch To place in cold water and bring to boil for a short time so as to remove the skin.

Cashew nuts Nuts from a tree mainly found in the coastal parts of tropical countries. Cashew nuts are bigger than peanuts and are white in colour. Your grocer will show you.

Cardamon Dark brown seeds used in certain Asian cookery as spices.

Cream of tartar Purified substance formed by completely fermented wine. The material is used for baking purposes.

Chestnut Fruit of a certain tree found in Spain. Your grocer will show you if in doubt.

Chilli Extremely hot pod which turns bright red when ripe and is used in certain Asian dishes as spices.

Cinnamon Inner bark of a certain tree growing mainly in the East Indies. The bark is ground into powder and used in cookery as spices.

Cloves Spices picked from trees grown in Zanzibar. In Swahili it is known as '*karafuu*'.

Coriander Seeds of a certain kitchen herb used as spices in some Asian dishes. Leaves are known as *dhania* or Chinese parsley.

Cumin powder (geera or jerra) Aromatic powder made from seeds of a certain plant and used as spices in some Asian dishes.

Curing Preserving by different methods.

Finger millet A tropical grain in the sorghum family. The stalk is about a foot high from the ground and the seeds are small, round and sometimes white in colour.

Garlic A plant in the onion family with a very strong flavour.

Ginger Root of a tropical plant used as spices in certain dishes.

Gut To remove the intestine of a fish when cleaning it ready for cooking.

Irio Kikuyu word. A mixture of maize, beans, potatoes and green vegetables cooked and mashed together.

Kebab Asian word. Pieces of meat threaded on to a skewer and roasted over open fire.
Pieces of vegetables and mushrooms could be put together with meat.

Kamongo Luo word. Mud fish or lung fish.

Karai Swahili word. An African type of a frying pan or a basin.

Kat-ayienya Luo word. Bubbling gravy or sauce. A mixture of melted ghee and a solution of bicarbonate of soda or sesquicarbonate.

Maize meal Maize flour or ground maize.

Mahu Kikuyu word. Tripe shaped like tubular bag.

Mara Kikuyu word. Small intestine of animal (or people).

Matoke Luganda word. Green banana which can be eaten. Plantains.

Monye Luo word (see kamongo).

Mustard A mixture of black and white seeds ground together and used in cooking for flavouring purposes.

Mutura Kikuyu word. Large intestine of animal used here to refer to dish made from stuffed and barbecued mutura.

Ngege Luo word. Tilapia from lake.

Nyoyo Luo word. A mixture of corn and beans, peas, or groundnuts.

Nutmeg Nut from a certain East Indies tree. The nuts are ground and used in cooking as spices.

Onyoso Luo word. An oily black tropical insect, caught in the day time during the rainy season in Western parts of Kenya.

Paprika Sweet red pepper known as Hungarian pepper.

Pepper Powder of a white pepper corn used in cookery for flavouring purposes.

Pepper-corn Berry of a vine grown mainly in East Indies, and used in certain dishes for flavouring purposes.

Pilau Asian word. A dish made with a mixture of rice and meat (chicken).

Raisins Dried grapes

Rissoles A mixture of minced meat (fish) with a paste such as mashed potatoes.

Roti Asian word. Another type of chapati.

Saffron Centre of a certain flower used on festive occasions to colour rice or curry dishes of Asian cooking.

Sage Kitchen herb used as spice for stuffing when roasting turkey.

Seasoning Flavouring materials—salt and pepper

Skewer A metal or wooden pin made for holding pieces of meat or vegetables when barbecueing or cooking over the open fire or under a grill.

Semutundu Luganda word. Mud fish or lung fish.

Senene Luganda word. (Senesene—Luo) Green grass-hopper usually caught at night during a certain period of the year.

These grasshoppers usually come in a swarm at night and flock round the lamp posts in towns, especially in Kampala.

Sesame (simsim) Small flat seeds which are creamy yellow in colour, oval shaped and have a crunchy nutlike flavour.

Souffle A dish prepared from the beaten whites of eggs.

Tumeric A deep yellow powder used in Asian dishes for colouring and flavouring.

Ugali Swahili word. African dish of stiff porridge served with any relish. It is a mixture of flour (of maize, millet, cassava or sorghum) and boiling water kneaded carefully with a wooden spoon over the fire.

Vinegar A sour liquid obtained from wine. It is usually added to certain European dishes for flavouring and preservation purposes.

Yam Root of a tropical climbing plant in the potato family.

Yoghourt Curdled milk usually flavoured.

AFRICAN RECIPES

MEAT

SMOKED MEAT (BILTONG) STEWED

4 servings

Ingredients

Meat 3 days old—enough for 4 people	4 spoonfuls ghee
2 medium sized onions	4 cupfuls water
2 medium sized tomatoes	Salt to taste

Method for smoking meat
1. Choose a lean piece of meat (beef, mutton or goat) and cut it into long pieces.
2. Fix some thin strong sticks on the wall above the fireplace, and hang the pieces of meat on the sticks. Leave the meat there for 3 days to enable it to dry.

Method for stewing
1. Wash meat thoroughly in cold water to remove the smoky taste.
2. Heat 1 spoonful ghee in a strong pan or pot with a tight-fitting lid.
3. Clean and slice onions and tomatoes and add them to the heated ghee. Fry into a sauce.
4. Cut meat into small pieces and add to the sauce.

5. Cook slowly, turning occasionally, until sauce gets absorbed into the meat. Add salt and water and simmer very slowly for about 2 hours until the meat is tender and just enough gravy remains.
6. When the meat is nicely cooked and the gravy tasty, add the remaining ghee and simmer again for about five minutes.
7. Remove from the heat and dish up in a clean bowl with a cover. Serve hot together with hot ugali.

Variations
   (a) All types of fish could be smoked and prepared in the same way but less water is required when cooking fish.
   (b) Smoking meat—if the housewife does not have a fireplace, she should make a fire-place within the compound, or else use a charcoal stove.
   (c) Ghee—home-made ghee is tastier but butter or any other cooking fat could be used.
   (d) Ugali—traditionally, smoked beef would be served with finger millet ugali but any other staple food such as steamed plantain will do.

MEAT IN COCONUT MILK

4 servings

Ingredients

Meat—beef or mutton enough for 4 people	2 medium sized tomatoes
	A little salad oil
3 cupfuls coconut milk	Water enough to cover the pan
1 large onion	Salt and curry powder to taste

Method
   1. Clean and cut meat into small pieces. Simmer in water for 2 hours until tender.
   2. Chop onions and tomatoes. Fry onion in a strong deep pan with salad oil and add tomatoes.
   3. Add meat, coconut milk and seasoning.
   4. Simmer slowly for about 30 minutes until gravy is thick and tasty.

   Serve hot with a staple food such as ugali, boiled rice, steamed plantains, cassava, or yams.

Variations
   (a) Any type of meat can be used, and even chicken or fish.
   (b) Add chopped tomatoes and onions instead of frying them. Simmer in coconut milk until they are ready. This way, coconut milk fat saves the use of salad oil.

MEAT AND VEGETABLE STEW

2 servings

Ingredients

Meat, soft cut or cold cooked enough for 2 people
1 cupful shelled peas
3 medium sized potatoes
1 small cabbage
2 medium sized tomatoes
2 spoonfuls margarine or other cooking fat
1 bunch small green onions
Salt and pepper to taste

Method
1. Chop meat into small pieces.
2. Wash, peel and cut the potatoes, cabbage, onions and tomatoes into small pieces.
3. Heat fat in a strong pan and add onions. Fry onions until a golden brown and add meat.
4. Fry meat until brown and then add vegetables and seasoning.
5. Cover with water and place lid on pan. Bring to the boil and then reduce heat. Simmer until meat is tender.

Place in a warm dish and serve immediately.

MEAT AND GREEN MAIZE STEW

2 servings

Ingredients

Chopped meat, enough for 2 people
1 cupful green maize off the cob
2 large onions
4 medium sized tomatoes
2 spoonfuls margarine or other cooking fat
Boiling water to cover maize in pan
Meat stock or water to cover meat

Method
1. Wash and clean maize and cook it in boiling water for about 30 minutes until soft. Chop onions and fry in a strong pan until they turn golden brown.
2. Add chopped meat and fry gently. Cover with water and add seasoning.
3. Chop tomatoes and add to the meat.
4. Add maize. Bring to the boil and reduce the heat.
5. Simmer until meat is tender.

Serve hot.

MEAT BARBECUE

4 servings

Ingredients
Lean, soft meat—boneless beef, mutton or veal—enough for 4 people
Salt and pepper to taste

Method
1. Beat the meat to make soft. Sprinkle over it salt and pepper. Cut it up into long thin pieces.
2. Make charcoal fire with no smoke. Place wire tray on top of fire. Spread meat on wire.
3. Turn pieces of meat every now and then so that the meat does not burn.
4. All parts of meat must be cooked.
5. Remove from charcoal fire and serve hot.

Eat with ugali, English potatoes, chipped or fried.

CHICKEN

CHICKEN STEW

6 servings

Ingredients
1 medium sized chicken
4 medium sized tomatoes
2 medium sized onions
2 spoonfuls cooking fat or oil
Salt and pepper to taste

Method
1. Clean and joint chicken.
2. Clean, peel and slice onions and fry in a strong pan until golden brown. Add chicken and fry well until nice and brown.
3. Wash tomatoes, slice and add to the chicken.
4. Add 1½ cups water and bring to the boil. Then reduce heat and cover with a tight fitting lid after seasoning.
5. Cook slowly until tender

   Serve hot with boiled rice or matoke or ugali or boiled cassava.

(CHICKEN IN EBINYEBWA) STEWED CHICKEN IN GROUNDNUT SAUCE

6 servings

Ingredients
1 medium sized boiler chicken
4 cupfuls groundnuts
2 medium sized onions
6 hard-boiled eggs 1 per person
Salt and pepper to taste.

Method
1. Clean chicken, joint it and cook the pieces in water for about 1 hour until soft.
2. Remove chicken from the stock.
3. Clean and roast groundnuts and then pound or crush.
4. Clean, chop and fry onion in a little oil.
5. Mix groundnut paste, onion and half of the stock. Add pieces of chicken and more stock if required. Add seasoning.
6. Simmer for 10 minutes. Add shelled boiled eggs and leave another 5 minutes.

7. Put in a dish with cover and serve hot with cold chopped tomatoes, onions and pineapple placed in separate small dishes.

Serve the chicken with boiled rice or any other staple food.

ROAST BONED CHICKEN

6 servings

Ingredients

Roasting chicken—enough for 6 people
8 medium sized chopped onions
8 large sized tomatoes
1 cupful peanut butter
2 spoonfuls breadcrumbs
A pinch cayenne pepper—optional
1 spoonful fat—approx.
1 spoonful flour—approx.

Method
1. Bone the chicken or ask your butcher to bone it if possible.
2. Fry the onion in the peanut butter and add tomatoes, crumbs, pepper and salt. This mixture is the stuffing.
3. Lay boned chicken flat on a board and sprinkle with salt.
4. Cover with prepared stuffing, and tie the chicken into a neat shape.
5. Cover with a little fat and sprinkle lightly with flour.
6. Roast in a moderately hot oven for about 1½ hours until crisp and golden brown.

Serve hot with steamed plantain, ugali or chipped potatoes.

FISH

NGEGE (FRIED LAKE FISH WITH GROUNDNUT SAUCE)

2 servings

Ingredients

1 big, or 2 small-sized ngege	1 cupful cooking oil
2 medium-sized onions	2 spoonfuls groundnut paste
2 spoonfuls curry powder, or any type of spices	Salt and pepper to taste
	1 cupful cold water

Method

1. Scale and gut the fish, then clean and wash it thoroughly and dry with cloth.
2. Cut the flesh across about ¼ inch deep in 3 places on both sides. Rub salt, pepper and curry powder into the cuts.
3. Heat oil in a strong large frying-pan or a karai until smoky hot. Put in fish and leave without turning until brown and crisp. Turn it to the other side and fry it the same way.
4. Reduce the heat and cover pan with a plate so that the inside of the fish is nicely cooked. Remove fish from pan and place in a flat dish. Keep hot.
5. Clean and slice onion and fry it quickly. Scatter it over the fish.
6. Remove pan from heat and put in groundnut paste and seasoning. Stir gently, adding cold water a little at a time while stirring. This will make the sauce.

7. Return to the heat and simmer gently until the sauce is thick and tasty.

   Serve at once with fish and ugali.

Variation
   Fish could be fried omitting the curry powder and eaten without any sauce.

FRIED FISH

4 servings

Ingredients
2 large or 4 small lake fish
6 spoonfuls peanut butter or ½
4 cupful oil
1 large sized chopped onion
8 medium sized skinned and chopped tomatoes
Salt and pepper to taste
2 spoonfuls flour

Method
1. Clean and wash the fish according to its kind.
2. Cut fish into four pieces and dry with a cloth.
3. Sprinkle with plenty of salt and pepper and toss in flour.
4. Heat oil or peanut butter in a clean frying pan smoking hot.
5. Fry fish in hot oil until golden brown on both sides for about 10 minutes in low fire.
6. Drain fish and keep hot.
7. Fry onions lightly in the hot fish fat. Add tomatoes and cook for about 5 minutes and season.
8. Arrange fish portion as a whole in a dish and lay onion and tomatoes mixture on top. Pour remaining butter or oil on top.

   Serve hot with ugali.

SMOKED "KAMONGO/MONYE" STEWED (SEMUTUNDU IN LUGANDA) (MUD FISH OR LUNG FISH)

6 servings

Ingredients

Dried piece of smoked kamongo/monye enough for 6
4-6 cupfuls fresh milk depending on hardness of fish
2 cupfuls ghee
2 large sized chopped onions
4 large sized chopped tomatoes
Salt to taste
Water as required

Method

1. Cut kamongo into serving pieces. Put in a strong pan and cover with water.
2. Scald by boiling kamongo in water for about 10 minutes.
3. Remove from the fire and pour away all the water.
4. Fry onions in two spoonfuls of ghee until well done.
5. Add tomatoes into the onion and mix well, cooking for about 5 minutes in the reduced heat.
6. Add pieces of fish and cook for about 10 minutes to allow tomato sauce to soak in, turning to prevent burning.
7. Add the remainder of ghee, milk and salt.
8. Simmer the fish slowly for about 2 hours, adding more milk if necessary. The fish should be tender and tasty when ready.
9. Remove from fire and serve hot with ugali.

Variations

(a) Any other type of smoked and dried fish could be prepared instead of kamongo but the cooking time should be reduced. Kamongo's flesh is usually tougher than other fish's flesh.
(b) Kamongo could be stewed in water first and then milk and ghee be added towards the end of cooking period. If water is used, the quantity of milk required will be less.
(c) Coconut milk could be used instead of cow's milk.
(d) Groundnut butter could be added in the middle of cooking to improve the flavour.
(e) Fresh kamongo could also be prepared by this method. If the fish is fresh, scalding is not required and cooking time is reduced from about 30 minutes to 1 hour depending on the age of kamongo.

FRIED FILLET OF KAMONGO/MONYE

6–12 servings depending on the fish size

Ingredients
1 whole fresh kamongo/monye	1 spoonful tumeric—vidhari
2–4 eggs	2 cupfuls oil or fat for frying
1 medium sized onion	Salt to taste
1 cupful wheat flour	

Method
1. Split kamongo/monye on the ventral side and gut it.
2. Remove the head, tail and the black skin, leaving only white meat.
3. Cut the meat across into serving pieces and shape them into meat fillets for frying. Wash the filletted parts of fish and dry with a piece of clean cloth.
4. Sprinkle some salt all over the fish taking care not to oversalt it.
5. Put flour in a wide plate and dip pieces of fish in flour rubbing well to dry all the water.
6. Heat the oil or fat in a roomy frying pan until the oil is smoky hot.
7. Beat eggs well in a roomy bowl and add tumeric and a little salt to taste. Beat again to dissolve the salt.
8. Dip pieces of fish in egg mixture and put into the hot oil to fry, putting as many pieces as could fit at the bottom of the pan. Make sure that you do not put one piece on top of the other.
9. Turn the pieces over as soon as the lower part turns golden brown, after about 3 minutes. Do not let it get burnt.
10. Let the other side turn brown and then reduce the fire to very low to prevent fish from burning.
11. Cover the pan and cook slowly for about 20 minutes until the inside of fish is thoroughly cooked. Remove from the fire and arrange neatly in a serving dish.
12. Serve hot with chipped potatoes and groundnut sauce with lemon, or with cheese sauce.

Variations
(a) Fry the pieces of fish on both sides until they turn golden brown, and then finish by baking in a slow oven until the inside of meat is thoroughly cooked.

(b) Tumeric could be rubbed on fish fillet before dipping the pieces into the beaten egg.
(c) Curry powder could be mixed with tumeric and the quantity increased as required.

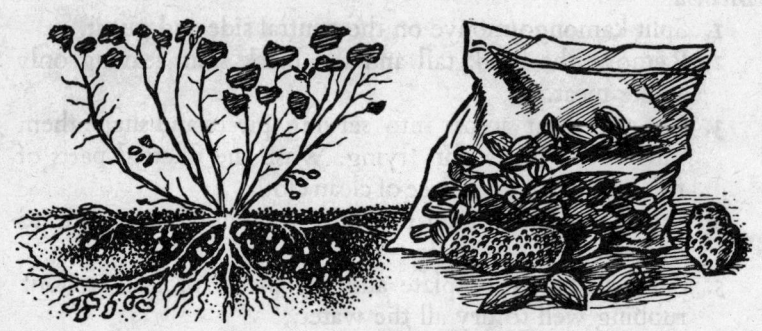

GROUNDNUT

EBINYEBWA (GROUNDNUT SAUCE)

4 servings

Ingredients
1 cupful shelled groundnuts
1 medium sized tomato
1 medium sized onion
1 teacupful milk
2 spoonfuls ghee
Salt to taste

Method
1. Roast groundnuts carefully, taking care not to burn them.
2. Allow to cool and pound them in a mortar, or grind them in a mincing machine into a paste.
3. Heat ghee in a strong saucepan and when hot add chopped onion and fry until golden brown.
4. Add chopped tomatoes. Stir the mixture until it turns into a paste.
5. Add groundnut paste and stir well until they are mixed thoroughly.

6. Add milk, stirring quickly to remove lumps, and add water to make mixture smooth.
7. Add salt and cover. Simmer on a slow fire for about 30 minutes, stirring occasionally.

Serve with steamed plantain or any of these: sweet potatoes, cassava, yams, boiled rice or ugali.

Variations
(a) Water could be used instead of milk.
(b) Groundnuts could be pounded before roasting and the sauce steamed instead of stewed.
(c) Cooked vegetables and chopped mushrooms could be added to the sauce.
(d) Juice of 1 lemon could be added and the sauce served with fried fish.

N.B. Steaming is done by putting a smaller pot containing the sauce inside the steam pot. Groundnut sauce can be added into main dishes such as stewed chicken, meat or stewed dried fish, in order to improve the flavour.

GROUNDNUT CAKES

6 servings

Ingredients
4 spoonfuls shelled groundnuts—peanuts
4 spoonfuls sugar
4 spoonfuls butter or margarine
4 spoonfuls water
2 spoonfuls sesame seeds—optional

Method
1. Roast peanuts in oven for about ½ hour. Cool and remove skin.
2. Boil sugar and butter in water until golden brown and thick like toffee.
3. Add peanuts and mix well, add sesame seeds.
4. Pour into buttered tin or place on a wet board and cut into 12 fancy shapes before the mixture becomes too cool and hardens.

Variation
(a) Use sesame seeds instead of groundnuts.

GROUNDNUT SOUP

6 servings

Ingredients

1 cupful roasted groundnuts
2 medium sized chopped onions
2 spoonfuls margarine
3 cupfuls water
3 cupfuls milk
Salt and pepper to taste

Method

1. Finely mince the groundnuts.
2. Melt margarine in a pan and fry chopped onions until soft. Add water to onions, bring to boiling point then reduce heat.
3. Add groundnuts and simmer for about 30 minutes or until sauce is thick.
4. Add milk and seasoning. Heat, but do not boil.

Serve hot with steamed cassava.

GROUNDNUT BREAD

12 servings

Ingredients

4 spoonfuls minced groundnuts
3 cupfuls flour
4 teaspoonfuls baking powder
½ teaspoonful salt
1½ cupfuls milk
2 spoonfuls sugar
1 egg

Method

1. Sieve flour, baking powder, salt and sugar into a bowl.
2. Beat the egg well and stir in the milk. Add the liquid to dry ingredients.
3. Add groundnuts and mix all thoroughly.
4. Grease a tin and then put in the mixture. Allow to stand for 20 minutes.
5. Bake for about 1 hour in moderately hot oven.
6. Remove from oven, cool on a rack and serve with tea.

GROUNDNUT BISCUITS

2 servings

Ingredients

1 cupful flour	4 spoonfuls margarine or butter
1 spoonful minced groundnuts	A little castor sugar
1 spoonful sugar	A little coarsely chopped groundnut for coating
1 egg	

Method
1. Put flour, groundnuts and sugar into a bowl. Work in margarine or butter with the fingers, kneading into a smooth paste.
2. Break the mixture into even pieces and dip them in beaten egg.
3. Coat with sugar and nuts.
4. Place on a greased baking tray, and bake for about 20 minutes until pale golden brown.
5. Remove from oven and cool on a rack.

Serve with tea.

MAIZE & MAIZE MEAL

UGALI (STIFF PORRIDGE)

4 servings

Ingredients
2 cupfuls maize flour, fresh and clean   4 cupfuls water

Method
1. Sieve the flour.
2. Boil water in a strong pan. Sprinkle flour into boiling water and stir with wooden spoon, adding flour little by little.
3. Stir and turn over again and again for about 20 minutes until mixture is thick and smooth. Make sure it is not too stiff. Add boiling water only if it is too thick.
4. Gather the mixture in the middle of the pan and turn heat low. Cover the pot and leave on low heat for 10-15 minutes.
5. Turn the mixture on to a plate and give it shape if necessary. Serve with relish such as stewed meat, fish, chicken, groundnut sauce, cooked vegetables, or even sour milk.

Variations
(a) Instead of maize flour, use any of these: millet flour, finger millet flour, cassava and sorghum flour, or maize and wheat flour.
(b) Use sour milk instead of water. This was done in the early days for preservation purposes during a journey, also in order to increase the nutrition value.

MAIZE FLOUR AND RICE FRIED

4 servings

Ingredients

½ cupful maize flour
½ cupful cold boiled rice
2 eggs
3 cupfuls sour milk
2 spoonfuls melted butter
½ teaspoonful bicarbonate of soda
1 spoonful hot water
2 spoonfuls fat or oil
Salt to taste

Method
1. Mix all above dry ingredients together except bicarbonate of soda.
2. Add well-beaten eggs and sour milk.
3. Dissolve bicarbonate of soda in hot water and add to mixture.
4. Grease a flat tin or frying pan with the fat, heat it and pour in mixture.
5. Turn over to cook other side, remove when ready after cooking for about 10 minutes, and serve hot.

GREEN MAIZE

6 servings

Ingredients

5 maize cobs
1½ cupfuls milk
Small lump butter
1 teaspoonful flour
3 cupfuls water
Salt and pepper to taste

Method
1. Remove maize grains off the cobs and put in a pot. Cover with water and cover pot with a tight-fitting lid. Boil for about 30 minutes until ready.
2. Remove from fire and drain away any remaining water.
3. Mix flour with milk, butter and seasoning and add grain.
4. Bring mixture to boil and cook for a further 10 minutes.

   Serve hot.

Variations
(a) GREEN MAIZE AU GRATIN—Add a little grated cheese to the above recipe. Place in a pie dish with more grated cheese

on top plus small pieces of butter. Bake in a moderately hot oven for about 10 minutes until brown, or brown under a grill for about 5 minutes.

(b) BAKED EGGS AND GREEN MAIZE—place mixture in pie dish and make a few holes in the surface. Break an egg into each hole and bake in a slow oven for about 15 minutes until eggs are cooked.

N.B. In African traditional cooking methods, green maize is always cooked by steaming method so that the water does not touch the cob, thereby making it tastier. Maize cobs are cooked as soon as they are picked from the garden so that the sweetness is not lost. Salt hardens the maize so it need not be added during cooking time.

CORN SOUP

6 servings

Ingredients
2 large fresh corn cobs
4 cupfuls milk
4 spoonfuls margarine
1 medium sized finely chopped onion
2 spoonfuls flour
Salt and pepper to taste

Method
1. Simmer corn steadily for about 20 minutes in one cupful of water.
2. Cool, then remove corn from the cob.
3. Heat half of the margarine in a pan and fry the finely chopped onions.
4. Stir in the flour and cook for about five minutes.
5. Add milk mixed with any little remaining liquid in which the corn was cooked. The liquid should be added gradually.
6. Bring to the boil, stirring to prevent burning.
7. Cook until thick and smooth.
8. Add corn and season with salt and pepper.

Re-heat and serve hot.

BAKED MAIZE AND EGGS

4 servings

Ingredients
1 cupful cooked green maize
2 eggs
3 spoonfuls butter
2 cupfuls milk
Salt and pepper to taste

Method
1. Beat eggs and milk together, then add butter and seasoning.
2. Mix with cooked maize and place in a greased pie-dish.
3. Bake in moderately hot oven for about 15 minutes until set and brown.

Remove from oven and serve.

BAKED MAIZE AND TOMATOES

4 servings

Ingredients
2 cupfuls cooked green maize grain
3 medium sized tomatoes
½ cupful breadcrumbs
A little butter
Salt and pepper to taste

Method
1. Butter a pie dish.
2. Pour boiling water over tomatoes, remove skins and slice.
3. Put a layer of sliced tomatoes followed by a layer of maize grains alternately in dish until full.
4. Sprinkle with salt and pepper and cover with breadcrumbs.
5. Place small pieces of butter on top and bake in hot oven for ½ hour.

Remove from oven and serve hot.

BROWN MAIZE MEAL BREAD

12 servings

Ingredients
2 cupfuls buttermilk	1 cupful white flour
½ cupful maize meal	½ cupful syrup or treacle
½ cupful sugar	½ teaspoonful bicarbonate of soda
2 cupfuls coarse brown meal or wholemeal flour	2 spoonfuls ground ginger

Method
1. Mix maize meal, sugar, coarse brown meal, ground ginger and flour together.
2. Warm up syrup or treacle and add buttermilk mixed with bicarbonate of soda.
3. Stir this into mixture of meal, sugar and flour.
4. Bake in moderately hot oven in a well-greased bread tin for 1½ hours.
5. Remove from the oven and place into a wire cooling tray. Serve cold with tea.

MAIZE FLOUR BREAD

6 servings

Ingredients
6 spoonfuls maize flour	1 teaspoonful salt
4 spoonfuls white flour	3 teaspoonfuls baking powder
2 spoonfuls sugar	2 eggs
2 spoonfuls margarine	1 cupful milk

Method
1. Sieve both flours and baking powder into a bowl. Add salt and sugar and mix well.
2. Beat egg thoroughly and add milk and melted margarine.
3. Pour liquid over the dry ingredients. Beat thoroughly with a wooden spoon.
4. Pour mixture into a well-greased shallow baking dish.

5. Bake until firm and golden brown for about 25 minutes using hot oven.
6. Turn out on to a wire cooling tray and serve hot or cold.

(MANDAZI) MAIZE DOUGHNUTS

6 servings

Ingredients

1 cupful maize flour	½ cupful white flour
1 egg	A little milk
2 spoonfuls sugar	A little oil

Method
1. Sieve the dry ingredients above into a bowl.
2. Beat the egg and stir lightly into dry ingredients.
3. Add enough milk to give a dropping consistency.
4. Heat a little oil in the pan, deep enough to cover the mixture when cooking. Drop a spoonful of mixture at a time into the fat and turn it over until it is golden brown.
5. Drain well by putting doughnuts on to soft clean paper and serve hot.

Variations
(a) White wheat flour could be used instead of maize flour. Cassava or millet flour could also be used.
(b) Honey or syrup could be used instead of sugar but it should be added to mixture with milk.

MAIZE PIE

6 servings

Ingredients

2 cupfuls green maize from the cob	2 spoonfuls flour
2 eggs	3 cupfuls milk
2 spoonfuls butter	Salt to taste

Method
1. Mince maize grain.
2. Heat butter and flour in a saucepan until smooth. Gradually add milk and bring to boil, then cool.
3. Add well beaten eggs and a pinch of salt.
4. Add minced grain and pour all into a greased pie dish.
5. Bake for about ½ hour in moderately hot oven until golden brown.

Serve hot.

MAIZE FLOUR BISCUITS

12 servings

Ingredients

2 cupfuls maize flour	6 spoonfuls margarine
1 cupful white flour	1 teaspoonful baking powder
6 spoonfuls sugar	

Method
1. Sieve maize flour, white flour and baking powder.
2. Cream sugar and margarine together. Add flour and mix well.
3. Form mixture into an even roll, and cut into slices.
4. Put on to a greased baking tray and bake in fairly hot oven until golden brown—about 15-20 minutes.

MAIZE MEAL BISCUITS

24 servings

Ingredients

3 cupfuls maize meal	8 spoonfuls sugar
2½ cupfuls white flour	1 egg
4 spoonfuls margarine or butter	1 teaspoonful bicarbonate of soda

Method
1. Remove grain from cobs and mince with onion and turnip.
2. Collect all the juice from the mincer and put in a saucepan with the boiling water adding mince mixture.
3. Cook for 1½ hours. Strain and add white sauce and perhaps a little cream.
4. Season with salt and pepper, garnish with chopped parsley and serve hot.

GREEN MAIZE AND MINCED CHICKEN

6 servings

Ingredients

3 cupfuls green maize, cut from cob
1 cupful minced, cooked chicken
1 spoonful cooked and chopped bacon

1 cupful white sauce
2 teaspoonfuls cream
2 eggs
Salt and pepper to taste

Method
1. Mince the raw green maize and the chicken separately. Then mix them together adding the chopped bacon.
2. Beat the whites of eggs well, and add both yolks and white sauce to them.
3. Add chicken mixture to egg mixture and season well.
4. Pour into a well-greased pie dish and bake for about 30 minutes until firm.
   Serve hot with tomato sauce.

GREEN MAIZE OMELETTE

6 servings

Ingredients

1½ cupfuls cooked green maize
4 eggs
1 egg white

4 spoonfuls milk
A little butter
Salt and pepper to taste.

Method
1. Melt margarine and mix in maize meal, flour, sugar and bicarbonate of soda.
2. Beat egg lightly and add to mixture.
3. Add enough water to make a stiff dough.
4. Roll out on a floured board and cut into shapes.
5. Bake on a slow oven for about 30 minutes until ready.

MAIZE IN MAYONNAISE

6 servings

Ingredients

1 cupful cooked maize grains
½ cupful mayonnaise sauce
A few leaves lettuce
1 spoonful butter
3 large-sized tomatoes
1 hard-boiled egg
Salt and pepper to taste

Method
1. To the cooked maize grains add mayonnaise, butter and seasoning.
2. Pour boiling water over tomatoes and remove skins. Scoop out the centre of each tomato and fill centres with maize mixture.
3. Serve on a bed of cut lettuce and sprinkle with chopped hard-boiled egg.

Variation
Firm baked potatoes or hard-boiled eggs may be substituted for tomatoes.

GREEN MAIZE SOUP

6 servings

Ingredients

5 green maize cobs
1 large sized onion
1 small sized turnip
2 cupfuls white sauce
8 cupfuls boiling water
Salt and pepper to taste

Method
1. Mince cooked green maize and add 3 well-beaten eggs, and one yolk, milk and seasoning.
2. Add the egg-white, well-beaten into a froth.
3. Fry in pan with butter, browning both sides.
4. Fold over and serve hot.

GREEN MAIZE CUSTARD

6 servings

Ingredients

1 cupful cooked green maize
2 cupfuls milk
3 eggs
A little chopped onion
Salt and pepper to taste

Method
1. Beat eggs slightly, and add to cooked and cooled maize.
2. Add chopped onion, seasoning and milk and mix together.
3. Pour into a buttered mould and bake for about 30 minutes until set.
4. Turn out and serve with tomato sauce.

MAIZE MEAL CAKE

6 servings

Ingredients

1 cupful maize flour
1 cupful white flour
2 teaspoonfuls baking powder
2 eggs
¼ cupful margarine
½ cupful sugar
¾ cupful milk
Salt to taste

Method
1. Mix and sift above dry ingredients.
2. Add well-beaten eggs and melted margarine, seasoning and milk. The milk should be just sufficient to make a good cake mixture.
3. Bake in a buttered tin until ready—about ¾ hour.

MAIZE MEAL SANDWICH CAKE

4 servings

Ingredients
4 eggs
Weight of the 4 eggs in butter
Weight of the 4 eggs in sugar
Weight of 2 eggs in white flour
Weight of 2 of the eggs in maize flour
1 teaspoonful baking powder
A little milk
flavouring if desired
A pinch of salt.

Method
1. Beat egg yolks and then the whites separately.
2. Beat butter and sugar together into a cream.
3. Add egg yolks and then add egg whites.
4. Mix baking powder, maize flour, white flour and a little salt.
5. Stir in the mixture gradually and add the flavouring.
6. Add milk and put into 2 greased sandwich tins.
7. Bake in a hot oven for about 20 minutes.
8. Cool, then spread jam or icing between sandwiches.

MAIZE MEAL DOUGHNUTS

12 servings

Ingredients
2 cupfuls white flour
1 cupful maize flour
1 cupful sugar
2 eggs
2 teaspoonfuls cream of tartar
1 teaspoonful bicarbonate of soda
A little milk
2 teaspoonfuls mixed spices
2 cupfuls oil

Method
1. Sieve both flours, sugar, bicarbonate of soda and mixed spices into a bowl.
2. Beat eggs with cream of tartar and stir gently into mixture.
3. Add a little milk to give good texture.
4. Heat the oil in a deep frying pan. Drop spoonfuls of the mixture, one at a time, into smoking oil. Turn so that the top is also cooked.

5. Remove from pan and roll in fine sifted sugar.

N.B. If sour milk is used instead of ordinary milk omit cream of tartar.

MAIZE MEAL DROP SCONES

6 servings

Ingredients
1 cupful white flour
½ cupful maize flour
1 teaspoonful baking powder
A little butter
4 spoonfuls sugar
1 egg
½ cupful milk
2 cupfuls—about—fat or oil

Method
1. Mix both flours together and add sugar, baking powder, well-beaten egg, butter and milk.
2. Mix well and drop in spoonfuls of the mixture on to a hot greased flat plate or electric hot-plate on top of stove. Cook on both sides.
3. Pile together on a clean cloth and keep covered until cool.

MAIZE MEAL FRITTERS

12 servings

Ingredients
2 cupfuls maize flour
1 cupful white flour
2 spoonfuls sugar
3 cupfuls milk
4 eggs
2 spoonfuls melted butter
½ teaspoonful bicarbonate of soda
1 teaspoonful cream of tartar
A pinch of salt
2 spoonfuls water—approx.
2 cupfuls oil—approx.

Method
1. Mix the flours, sugar and salt together.
2. Dissolve bicarbonate of soda in a very little water.
3. Stir into mixture well-beaten egg yolks, melted butter milk, cream of tartar, bicarbonate of soda, and lastly, well-beaten whites of eggs.

4. Mix all thoroughly and cook in very hot oil as for doughnuts. (See page 41.)
5. When cooked, remove and place on soft paper to absorb fat. Serve as a pudding with any sauce.

MAIZE MEAL ROCK CAKES

4 servings

Ingredients
3 spoonfuls maize flour
3 spoonfuls white flour
2 spoonfuls margarine
1 spoonful currants
3 spoonfuls sugar
1 teaspoonful baking powder
1 egg
A little milk

Method
1. Mix the flours together and rub in margarine. Add sugar, baking powder, beaten eggs and currants.
2. Mix well and add a little milk if required at all.
3. See that the mixture is not soft.
4. Grease an oven tin and put in mixture in rough lumps.
5. Bake in hot oven for 15 minutes.

Serve hot or cold.

MAIZE MEAL ROLLS

24 servings

Ingredients
1½ cupfuls maize flour
2 cupfuls white flour
4 spoonfuls sugar
1 cupful milk
1 egg
4 teaspoonfuls baking powder
½ teaspoonful salt
4 spoonfuls margarine

Method
1. Sieve together both flours, baking powder, salt and sugar.
2. Add well-beaten egg, melted margarine and milk.
3. Mix all well together and put two spoonfuls of mixture in a small greased tin.

4. Do this until mixture is used up.
5. Bake tins in oven for 35 minutes.

   Serve hot with butter.

MAIZE PANCAKES

6 servings

Ingredients

2 cupfuls green maize grain
4 spoonfuls white flour
½ cupful cream
4 spoonfuls sugar
4 eggs
A pinch salt
Fat or oil as required for cooking

Method
1. Mince green maize grains.
2. Beat yolks of eggs and whites of eggs separately.
3. Mix together the yolks of eggs, minced grain, flour and cream, and lastly add egg whites.
4. Drop spoonfuls of this mixture into a hot greased frying pan.
5. Cook on both sides for about 5 minutes until ready.
6. Serve as pudding with any sauce.

Variations
(a) The sugar could be omitted and then the dish could be served with meat.
(b) Two spoonfuls of melted butter mixed with a little milk could be used instead of cream.

CORN SCONES

6 servings

Ingredients

6 spoonfuls maize flour
2½ spoonfuls wheat flour
2 teaspoonfuls baking powder
½ teaspoonful salt
2 spoonfuls sugar
1 cupful milk
1 egg
2 spoonfuls margarine

Method

1. Sieve all dry ingredients above into a bowl.
2. Beat egg, milk and salt thoroughly.
3. Add egg and milk mixture to the dry ingredients and mix with wooden spoon.
4. Melt margarine and beat it into mixture.
5. Grease individual small tins and fill them two-thirds full with mixture.
6. Bake in a very hot oven for about 20 minutes.

Serve well-buttered, cold or hot.

MAIZE MEAL PUDDING

12 servings

Ingredients

5½ cupfuls milk
2 cupfuls maize meal
½ cupful castor sugar
1 cupful white flour
4 eggs

1 spoonful mixed spices
2 spoonfuls butter
½ teaspoonful soda bicarbonate
1 teaspoonful cream of tartar

Method

1. Mix maize meal and flour.
2. Boil milk and stir carefully into maize meal and flour. Boil for 10 to 15 minutes, stirring all the time to prevent scorching.
3. Add butter, remove from heat and beat well.
4. Leave to cool, then add eggs, one at a time beating thoroughly.
5. Add sugar, spices, bicarbonate of soda and cream of tartar.
6. Bake in well-greased small tins for about 30 minutes until well-cooked.

Serve with cream or any other pudding sauce.

MAIZE MEAL SPONGE

6 servings

Ingredients

1 cupful white flour
½ cupful maize meal
½ cupful sugar
1 cupful sour milk

2 yolks of egg
1 white of egg
2 spoonfuls melted butter
½ teaspoonful soda bicarbonate

Method
1. Mix flour, maize meal, sugar, bicarbonate of soda together.
2. Stir in melted butter, sour milk and yolks of eggs which have been well beaten.
3. Beat the egg white stiffly into a froth and add to mixture.
4. Grease a sandwich tin and pour in mixture.
5. Bake in a hot oven for about 1 hour until ready.

SWEET POTATO

SWEET POTATOES IN COCONUT MILK

2 servings

Ingredients
1 whole coconut
4 medium sized sweet potatoes
Salt to taste

Method
1. Wash and peel sweet potatoes and cut into pieces.
2. Make coconut milk in usual way and bring to boiling point in a clean pan. Add potatoes and salt and cover with a tight-fitting lid.
3. Boil slowly until potatoes are tender. Remember to save some coconut milk for adding into potatoes in case they dry up in cooking.
4. Remove from heat.

   Serve hot with groundnut sauce, vegetable sauce or any relish.

Variation

Use any other root vegetable, such as cassava, yams, English potatoes or plantains. If cassava is used make sure that the middle string is removed before cooking.

SWEET POTATO CHIPS

2 servings

Ingredients
2 large-sized sweet potatoes   A little salad oil or cooking oil
                                    Salt to taste

Method
1. Peel sweet potatoes and cut into fingers as for chips.
2. Wash thoroughly and drain.
3. Heat oil in a deep pan until smoking hot and drop chips in a few at a time.
4. Turn over chips frequently until crisp and brown.
5. Remove from oil and sprinkle with salt then drain on clean soft paper.

Serve very hot with groundnut sauce, coconut sauce or bean sauce.

Variations
(a) Arrow-roots, cassava or yams could be used in place of sweet potatoes.
(b) A more economical method using less oil is first to half-cook the peeled potatoes—or the others as above—by putting them into salty water and bring to boil.

Drain off water, cut into chips and heat as above.

SWEET POTATO CAKE

4 servings

Ingredients
2 medium sized sweet potatoes   1 teaspoonful salt
2 spoonfuls flour   ¼ teaspoonful pepper
1 spoonful margarine   A little fat

Method
1. Peel, wash, cook and mash sweet potatoes.
2. Mix potatoes with salt, pepper and melted margarine, then beat in flour to form a stiff dough.

3. Roll out to ½ inch thickness and cut into 4 pieces.
4. Fry on greased hot plate or frying pan and remove when golden brown.

Serve on warm plate with any relish.

SWEET POTATO BREAD

6 servings

Ingredients

1 cupful cooked mashed, sweet potatoes
1 cupful maize flour
1 cupful white flour
2 teaspoonfuls baking powder
A little milk

Method

1. Mix all ingredients together using only sufficient milk to make a stiff mixture.
2. Bake in hot oven for about 30 minutes until ready.

Serve hot or cold.

SWEET POTATOES BAKED IN BUTTER

4 servings

Ingredients

4 medium sized sweet potatoes
½ cupful melted butter
4 spoonfuls sugar
Salt and pepper to taste

Method

1. Peel and boil potatoes and then cool.
2. Slice them length-wise and dip in butter mixed with sugar.
3. Lay them in baking pan in a very hot oven.
4. Leave to cook to a nice brown for about 30 minutes.

Serve hot.

SWEET POTATOES WITH TOMATOES

4 servings

Ingredients

2 medium-sized sweet potatoes   ½ teaspoonful sugar
2 spoonfuls margarine   Salt and pepper and chilli
3 medium-sized tomatoes   powder to taste.

Method
1. Wash and peel potatoes and then boil.
2. Skin and slice tomatoes.
3. Allow potatoes to cool, then slice them.
4. Melt margarine and fry sliced potatoes for about 5 minutes until golden brown.
5. Add seasoning and sugar.
6. Add tomatoes and cook for about 5 minutes until tender.

   Serve hot.

SWEET POTATO SAUSAGES

4 servings

Ingredients

1 packet sausage meat—8 pieces   Oil for frying
2 cupfuls grated sweet potatoes   1 teaspoonful salt

Method
1. Grate raw sweet potatoes.
2. Mix them with salt and sausage meat and form into flat round cakes.
3. Heat oil and fry cakes for about 5 minutes until golden brown on both sides.

   Serve hot.

SWEET POTATO CHEESE AND ONION CASSEROLE

4 servings

Ingredients
2 medium-sized sweet potatoes
2 large-sized onions
1 cupful grated cheese
Salt, pepper and chilli powder to taste

Method
1. Peel and slice thinly sweet potatoes.
2. Peel and slice onions. Grate cheese.
3. Grease a fireproof dish and put the potatoes, onions and cheese in layers in dish. Add seasoning to taste.
4. Cover top of dish with liberal layer of grated cheese.
5. Cover with lid and bake on moderately hot oven for 1 hour.
6. Remove lid, then brown under grill.

   Serve hot.

FRIED SWEET POTATO BALLS

6 servings

Ingredients
1 large-sized sweet potato per person
5 spoonfuls sugar
4 spoonfuls flour
1 egg
1 cupful sesame—simsim—seeds
A little oil

Method
1. Steam sweet potatoes until very soft.
2. Strain, peel and mash them until smooth.
3. Cool, then mix with sugar and egg.
4. Form mixture into even sized balls.
5. Mix flour and a little water together into a soft batter then add simsim seeds.
6. Heat oil in a pan until smoky hot. Dip balls into the batter and fry until golden brown.
7. Lift from oil and drain on soft paper.

   Serve as required.

CASSAVA

BAKED CASSAVA AND SWEET CORN

4 servings

Ingredients
1 small sized cassava
3 eggs
4 spoonfuls roasted and chopped groundnuts
1 roasted sweet corn cob
1 cupful milk
8 spoonfuls margarine

Method
1. Remove corn from cob. Melt margarine and add corn and groundnuts.
2. Boil cassava for about 30 minutes and slice thinly.
3. Line a greased pie dish with sliced cassava and cover with corn and groundnuts.
4. Beat eggs and add milk and seasoning.
5. Pour over corn and nuts and bake for about 20 minutes until ready.

Serve hot.

CASSAVA CHEESE BALLS IN BATTER

4 servings

Ingredients
1 small cassava
½ cupful grated cheese
1 well beaten egg
A little oil
Salt and pepper to taste

Batter Recipe
¼ cupful flour
2 spoonfuls baking powder
A little water

Method
1. Peel, cut and cook the cassava in boiling water for about 30 minutes until soft.
2. Mash together the cassava, cheese, beaten egg and seasoning.
3. Put a little flour on the hands and form mixture into even-sized balls.
4. Mix batter recipe together and beat until smooth.
5. Heat oil in frying pan until very hot. Dip each ball into batter and lower gently into hot oil.
6. Cook for about 5 minutes or until batter is brown and crisp.
7. Lift out, drain off oil and serve hot.

CASSAVA CHEESE PIE

4 servings

Ingredients

1 medium sized cassava	1 cupful milk
½ cupful grated cheese	2 medium sized carrots
2 spoonfuls margarine	Salt to taste

Method
1. Scrub cassava, peel and cut into small pieces. Boil it in salted water for about 30 minutes until tender.
2. Scrub and peel carrots and cook.
3. Mash cassava until free from lumps.
4. Add milk, margarine and three-quarters of grated cheese and the seasoning.
5. Mix thoroughly and beat until white and fluffy.
6. Put in greased fireproof dish and sprinkle with remaining grated cheese.
7. Cut carrots into thin circles to decorate pie on top.
8. Bake or brown under grill.

Serve hot.

SAVOURY CASSAVA BISCUITS

12 servings

Ingredients

2 spoonfuls margarine
3 cupfuls cooked and mashed cassava
2 cupfuls flour
12 spoonfuls grated cheese
Salt and pepper to taste

Method
1. Sieve flour and rub margarine into it.
2. Add mashed cassava and cheese. Season to taste.
3. Work into a dough with the hands. Roll out thickly and cut into round pieces using a tumbler upside down.
4. Put on a greased baking tray and bake until ready (about 15-20 minutes).

CASSAVA CAKES

6 servings

Ingredients

2 cupfuls cooked and mashed cassava
1 cupful grated cheese
4 spoonfuls flour
1 medium sized onion thinly sliced
A little oil or fat
Salt and pepper to taste.

Method
1. Mix mashed cassava with flour and add seasoning.
2. Roll out on to a floured board and cut into rounds.
3. Heat oil in frying pan and fry until cassava and flour is golden brown.
4. Coat rings of onion with grated cheese and place one on top of each cake.
5. Put under grill to melt cheese until golden brown.

   Arrange in a plate and serve hot.

CASSAVA SCONES—QUICK METHOD

6 servings

Ingredients
1 cupful cassava, boiled and mashed
½ cupful flour
A little oil or fat
1 teaspoonful baking powder
Salt to taste

Method
1. Put all ingredients into bowl and knead until it forms into a ball.
2. Roll out onto a floured board and cut into rounds.
3. Fry until ready.

Serve hot with poached eggs for breakfast.

CASSAVA SCOTCH EGGS

4 servings

Ingredients
½ cupful boiled and mashed cassava
4 hard-boiled eggs
1 egg
A little oil
A little minced groundnuts
Salt and pepper to taste

Method
1. Beat mashed cassava with seasoning and divide into 4 evensized portions.
2. Cover the 4 hard-boiled eggs with cassava mixture.
3. Beat the remaining egg. Dip the cassava eggs into beaten egg and roll into groundnuts, coating each one completely.
4. Heat oil and fry until golden brown.
5. Drain off oil and cut each in half lengthwise.

Serve hot or cold with salad.

CASSAVA FLOUR ROLLS

6 servings

Ingredients
1 cupful cassava fllour
1 spoonful brown sugar
2 teaspoonfuls sugar
4 teaspoonfuls baking powder
3 spoonfuls raisins
3 spoonfuls fat

1 egg
1 cupful milk
3 spoonfuls butter or margarine
2 spoonfuls brown sugar
Salt and any spice to sprinkle on top of rolls

Method
1. Soak raisins in water. After 15 minutes, remove from water and dry.
2. Sieve flour, salt and baking powder into bowl, and add 2 teaspoonsful of sugar.
3. Chop fat and rub it into flour with tips of fingers.
4. Beat the egg then pour into milk and mix, until soft but not sticky.
5. Flour the board lightly and roll dough.
6. Spread lightly with butter or margarine and sprinkle with brown sugar, dry raisins and cinnamon if desired.
7. Damp the edges and roll up.
8. Cut into slices and place close together on a baking sheet.
9. Bake in a hot oven for about 20 minutes until ready.

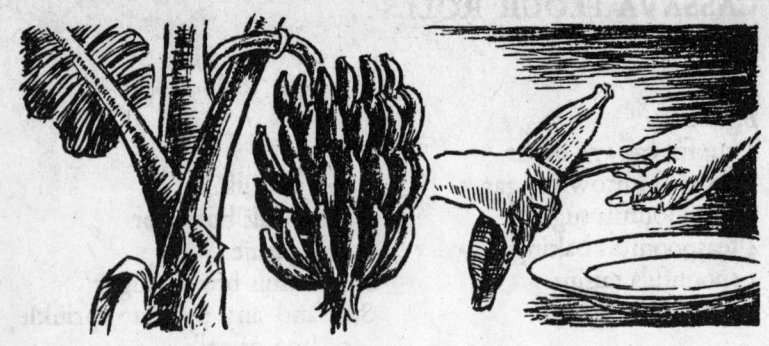

MATOKE

STEAMED MATOKE WITH STEWED CHICKEN

6 servings

Ingredients
6 green plantains per person
1 whole roasting chicken
2 medium sized tomatoes
½ cupful flour
1 medium sized onion
½ cupful ghee
Curry powder to taste
Salt and pepper to taste
2 cupfuls water

Method
1. Peel plantain and wash in cold water.
2. Using aluminium foil or two large clean banana leaves, tie up the plantain into a neat package secured with a clean piece of string or banana fibres.
3. At the bottom of a large saucepan or pot place clean wooden stick or the midrib of banana leaves as a support. Just cover them with cold water.
4. Place the package of plantain on the support. Cover with another aluminium foil or banana leaf tucking the ends into the pot. Steam gently for about an hour.
5. Clean and cut chicken into small pieces and dip them into flour.
6. Fry in hot ghee until golden brown. Remove from the pan.
7. Slice onion and tomatoes and fry. Return the pieces of chicken into the pan.

8. Add two cups of water and seasoning. Simmer until tender, for about 30 minutes.
9. Remove package of matoke from the pot and place on large plate or tray. Press with the hands at all sides of package until plantain becomes a soft mash.
10. Remove the aluminium foil or banana leaves and return to the pot and leave over a slow heat for about 30 minutes to 1 hour until the colour is golden brown.
11. Serve piping hot and to keep the heat, cover with foil or a hot banana leaf. Remove chicken from pan and serve hot with the matoke.

NOTE: Plantain must not be allowed to ripen before cooking. This dish must be served hot as the matoke will become hard and unpalatable if allowed to cool.

MATOKE COOKED IN MILK

4 servings

Ingredients
16 plantains
Milk—sufficient to cover
Salt and pepper to taste

Method
1. Peel the 10 matoke, cut into thick slices and wash.
2. Put them into a pan, cover with milk and add seasoning.
3. Cook over a gentle heat for about 30 minutes until soft.

Serve hot with any relish.

BROWNED MATOKE

4 servings

Ingredients
10 matoke
3 spoonfuls margarine
1 large sized chopped onion
Salt and pepper to taste

Method
1. Peel and wash, then boil the matoke whole until tender.
2. Melt margarine and fry chopped onions to golden brown.

3. Add matoke into margarine and onion and break into small pieces using fork or spoon.
4. Add seasoning, mix well then cover pan with a lid.
5. Reduce heat and cook slowly for about 15 minutes until browned.
6. Turn out into a deep dish and serve hot with any relish.

CRISPIE MATOKE

4 servings

Ingredients
10 steamed matoke A little chopped groundnuts
½ cupful melted margarine Salt and pepper to taste

Method
1. Drain steamed matoke then place into melted margarine.
2. Roll each matoke in chopped groundnuts, sprinkle with seasoning, then cook on a baking tray in oven for about 15 minutes.

Serve hot.

MATOKE CAKE SANDWICHES WITH MINCED MEAT

4 servings

Ingredients
1 cupful mashed matoke Salt and pepper to taste
4 spoonfuls flour

Meat Filling
1 cupful minced meat
1 egg
1 medium sized chopped onion
1 slice crumbled bread
Salt and pepper to taste

Method for Matoke cake Sandwiches
1. Mix all above ingredients together into a bowl.
2. Turn out on to floured board and roll out flat.
3. Cut into rounds, fry and keep warm.

Method for Meat Filling
1. Mix onion, crumbled bread and seasoning with egg.
2. Fry meat until ready then add to the mixture and keep stirring while cooking.
3. Form into flat, round cake the same size as the matoke rounds.

   Spread the mixture between two matoke cakes and serve hot.

DEEP-FRIED MATOKE CHIPS

6 servings

Ingredients
Matoke—as required, allowing 2-3 per person
2 cupfuls fat or oil

Method
1. Peel and wash any number of matoke.
2. Cut into finger sizes and dry in a cloth.
3. Heat oil or fat in a strong deep frying pan until smoking hot.
4. Put chipped matoke into fat and cook for about 5 minutes until soft and pale brown.
5. Remove from pan and place on soft paper to drain away oil.
6. Serve quickly while hot.

Variations
(a) Matoke sticks or straws—These are prepared in the same way as chips but the matoke are cut into thinner sticks.
(b) Matoke Crisps—as above but the matoke are cut into very thin rounds.

MATOKE WITH BEANS

2 servings

Ingredients
4 matoke   1 spoonful margarine
4 spoonfuls beans   Salt and pepper to taste

Method
1. Soak beans in water until soft, then drain and clean.
2. Peel and dice matoke and wash in cold water.
3. Mix beans with matoke and cook in very little water until tender or until water dries up.
4. Add margarine and seasoning, then mash.

Heat and serve hot.

COCONUT

TUI YA NAZI (COCONUT MILK)

Method
1. Break coconut into halves by knocking it against a hard surface. See that the white flesh is clean—wash it if necessary.
2. Remove the white flesh from the nut by scraping it out. It will break into pieces.
3. Grate these pieces on a cheese grater. Cover the result with warm water and soak for about ½ hour.
4. Strain through a fine clean sieve or muslin cloth.

COCONUT RICE

4 servings

Ingredients

2 coconuts
1 cupful rice
4 medium sized tomatoes
1 small sized onion
Salt and pepper to taste

Method
1. Clean and wash rice. Soak it in water for about 30 minutes.
2. Make coconut milk in the usual way and bring it to the boil.
3. Drain water from rice. Add rice and seasoning to coconut milk, stirring occasionally while cooking to prevent from burning.
4. When rice is cooked after about 30 minutes, allow coconut milk to dry out, then put it into fireproof dish and place in oven.

   Remove from the oven, and serve with stewed meat, chicken, fish or groundnut sauce.

N.B. If there is no oven, put some burning charcoal on to a clean tin and cover dish with hot tin. This will allow water to evaporate and rice grains to separate.

Variations
(a) Rice can be half-boiled in water first before adding coconut milk. In this case less coconut milk will be required.
(b) Soft pieces of meat could be added to coconut milk before adding rice. This makes the dish a complete meal.

COCONUT SAUCE

4 servings

Ingredients

1 coconut
½ cupful beans
1 small onion
1 small tomato
A little salad oil
Seasoning to taste

Method
1. Clean and wash beans.

2. Boil in water for about 1 hour until tender, then remove from heat. Mash and pass through a fine sieve.
3. Clean and chop onion and tomato. Fry them in salad oil or other cooking fat. Add beans and stir.
4. Add milk from the coconut previously prepared.
5. Season and cook slowly stirring occasionally for about 10 minutes.

   Serve with one of the following: steamed plantain, sweet potatoes, cassava, boiled rice or ugali.

Variations

   Onion, tomato and salad oil could be omitted altogether. Prepare as above but add more coconut milk and serve as soup instead of sauce.

N.B. Coconut sauce can also be served as an accompaniment to any fried fish dish.

COCONUT SALAD

6 servings

Ingredients

1 freshly grated coconut   1 lettuce heart

Method
1. Wash lettuce heart and then dry.
2. Put into a glass dish and sprinkle with clean grated coconut.
3. Serve with mayonnaise sauce.

COCONUT CONES

6 servings

Ingredients

1½ cupfuls grated coconut   2 spoonfuls flour
½ cupful castor sugar   2 egg whites

Method
1. Beat the whites of eggs well.
2. Mix sugar, coconut and flour together and add egg white mixture.

3. Fill wetted egg cups with mixture and turn them out on to a greased baking tin.
4. Bake in a moderately hot oven for about 15 minutes.
5. Cool and serve as required.

COCONUT BISCUITS

6 servings

Ingredients

2 cupfuls flour
2 cupfuls grated coconut
1 egg
6 spoonfuls castor sugar
4 spoonfuls margarine or butter
A little milk

Method
1. Mix all ingredients together in a bowl. Work in the margarine or butter by hand.
2. Add a little milk if too thick and then roll and cut into rounds.
3. Put on a floured baking sheet and bake in a slow oven for about 20 minutes until light brown.
4. Cool and serve as required.

COCONUT AND SWEET POTATO PUDDING

6 servings

Ingredients

1 cupful freshly grated coconut
1½ cupfuls sweet potatoes, boiled or mashed
2 eggs
¾ cupful sugar
¾ cupful milk
½ cupful water
4 spoonfuls melted butter
½ teaspoon mixed spices
½ teaspoon cinnamon

Method
1. Mix sugar, sweet potatoes and coconut together with a spoon until smooth.
2. Add butter, milk and water and beat thoroughly.
3. Beat the eggs slightly, then beat in the mixture gradually.

4. Add spices and cinnamon. Continue beating until creamy and very smooth.
5. Put into a greased fireproof dish and bake for about 30 minutes in a hot oven, until golden brown.

Serve hot or cold.

COCONUT PUDDING

6 servings

Ingredients

1 coconut	2 spoonfuls sugar
4 eggs	¼ teaspoonful salt
3 cupfuls milk	

Method
1. Grate coconut finely, and mix with sugar and eggs. Beat thoroughly until light and fluffy.
2. Gradually add milk, mixing well until it is smooth.
3. Pour mixture into a greased baking tin. Sprinkle a little grated coconut over the top.
4. Bake in a moderately hot oven for about 30 minutes until firm and set.

Serve either hot or cold.

MIXTURES

IRIO (MAIZE AND BEAN MASH)

6 servings

Ingredients
4 green maize cobs   4 medium sized potatoes
2 cupfuls beans   2 bunches pumpkin leaves
Salt to taste

Method
1. Remove maize grain from cobs (See page 37) and boil with beans until soft.
2. Peel potatoes, wash, and add to the grain together with pumpkin leaves and boil together until potatoes are cooked.
3. Drain, add salt and mash.

Variations
(a) For fried irio, prepare as above but add curry powder, stirring well into onions.
(b) For curried irio, chop about 4 medium sized onions and fry in 2 spoonfuls fat until brown. Add 2 spoonfuls curry powder and stir well. Add irio and simmer for 5 minutes. Serve hot.
(c) Meat may be added but it should be mashed.

NYOYO (BEANS AND BOILED MAIZE)

6 servings

Ingredients

2 cupfuls green maize off the cob
1 small, finely chopped onion
1 cupful beans
2 spoonfuls margarine or butter
½ spoonful salt

Method
1. Wash beans, removing all dirt. Cover with water and half cook, adding only boiling water when necessary.
2. Clean and wash maize and add to the beans. Cook beans and maize until tender.
3. Fry onion with one spoonful of margarine until golden brown.
4. Add maize and beans and salt and mix well. Add remaining margarine and cover. Allow margarine to soak for 10 minutes.

Serve hot.

Variations
(a) African peas or green grams could be used in place of beans.
(b) Dried maize off the cob could be used instead of green maize but it should be soaked first and then half-cooked before adding the vegetable.
(c) Onions and margarine may be omitted. If so the dish is served as soon as the cooking is done.

RICE AND BEAN STEW

4 servings

Ingredients

1 cupful rice
1 cupful beans
Oil and onions if desired
Salt to taste

Method
1. Clean and wash beans and boil in salty water until nearly cooked.
2. Clean and wash rice and mix into beans.

3. When nearly cooked add oil and onion and then reduce heat and allow to simmer.
4. Remove from heat and serve hot with coconut sauce or groundnut sauce—ebinyebwa.

Variations
(a) Use other pulses such as green grams or cow peas instead of beans.
(b) Omit oil from the dish.

DENGU (GREEN GRAM SAUCE)

4 servings

Ingredients
1 cupful green grams
2 medium sized onions
½ cupful cooking oil
2 cupfuls milk
4 spoonfuls ghee or butter
Salt and curry powder to taste

Method
1. Clean and wash green grams. Place in pot, cover with water and boil until very tender. If more water needed, add only boiling water.
2. Remove from heat and beat until smooth. It will turn into a paste.
3. Put green gram paste into a bowl and heat cooking oil in same pot.
4. Clean and dice onions. Add onions to oil and fry until cooked and nicely brown.
5. Return the green gram paste to the pot and mix with onion.
6. Add curry powder, salt and milk and simmer for 10 minutes.
7. Add butter or ghee and simmer for another 5 minutes.
8. Remove from heat and place in clean dish with cover.

Serve hot with boiled rice, boiled sweet potatoes, steamed plantain, boiled cassava, or ugali made from maize flour.

SOYA BEANS WITH GREENS
4 servings

Ingredients

1 cupful soya beans
1 bunch green vegetables
1 large sized onion
2 spoonfuls oil or fat
Salt to taste

Method
1. Wash and boil beans until soft for about one hour.
2. Clean, prepare and boil the greens in salty water for about 15 minutes.
3. Remove both beans and greens from the fire.
4. Chop onions and fry in a clean pan.
5. Add both beans and greens and mix well.
6. Cook for about 5 minutes to let the oil soak in well. Add more salt if required.
7. Serve hot with ugali or steamed plantain.

Variations

(a) Greens could be prepared in the same way as explained above and then soya flour added to the greens instead of cooked beans. If this method is preferred, allow one cup of soya flour to four cups of water. Onions are fried and added to the mixture but the sauce should be cooked slowly for about 30 minutes to reduce the liquid.

(b) Cooked mushrooms could be added to the green vegetable mixture.

SOYA BEAN SCONES
10-12 servings

Ingredients

1 cupful soya flour
4 cupfuls wheat flour
1 egg
2 spoonfuls sugar
1 cupful fat or oil for frying
1 teaspoonful salt
A little milk or water as required.

Method
1. Mix the flour with soya flour and salt.
2. Beat up the egg and sugar and stir into the flour.

3. Add a little milk or water to make a dough.
4. Heat fat or oil over a slow fire in a strong frying pan.
5. Drop a spoonful of the mixture into the hot fat and fry on both sides until well cooked for about 10 minutes on both sides.
6. Remove from heat and drop the rest until all mixture is cooked.
7. Serve hot or cold with tea.

FINGER MILLET FLOUR PORRIDGE

6 servings

Ingredients
6 spoonfuls finger millet flour
2 spoonfuls sugar
2 cupfuls milk
2 cupfuls water

Method
1. Blend flour gradually into water, using a little water at a time.
2. Add milk and bring to boil slowly, stirring frequently and gently—using a strong pan.
3. Add sugar and continue cooking for about 15 minutes.

Serve when ready.

Variations
(a) Sour milk was traditionally used, instead of fresh milk.
(b) Any kind of flour could be used, instead of finger millet flour.
(c) Water could be boiled first in a strong saucepan and then the flour mixed with milk and added to the boiling water.
(d) The milk could be left out when cooking, but added at table.

AFRICAN SPINACH IN MILK

6 servings

Ingredients
2 bundles African spinach
4 spoonfuls cooking oil
2 medium sized onions
1 cupful milk

1 cupful boiling water
4 spoonfuls butter, margarine or ghee
1 teaspoonful salt

Method
1. Prepare and clean spinach, washing it in cold water, then drain.
2. Put the cup of boiling water in a pot with a tight-fitting lid and add salt and spinach. Cover tightly and boil quickly for 20 minutes, turning after 10 minutes. All the water should dry up.
3. Remove spinach from the heat and take out of pot.
4. Chop onions. Heat oil in the pot and add onions. Fry and keep turning until they are nicely cooked.
5. Add spinach and turn it in hot oil for about 10 minutes, until onion is properly mixed. Make sure the spinach does not burn.
6. Add milk and butter, margarine or ghee, and simmer for 2 minutes.

Serve hot with any type of ugali or steamed plantain.

Variations
(a) African spinach—any kind of spinanch could be used instead.
(b) Pounded groundnut paste could be added either with milk or instead of milk.
(c) Milk or groundnut paste could be added without frying the vegetable. Oil and onions would not then be required.
(d) Spices, such as curry powder, could be added.

VEGETABLES IN COCONUT MILK

6 servings

Ingredients

2 bunches African spinach	1 medium sized tomato
1 large coconut	1 cupful water
1 medium sized onion	Salt and curry powder to taste

Method
1. Prepare and clean spinach. Chop onion and tomato.
2. Boil water and add salt. Add prepared spinach, cover and boil quickly, turning it over from time to time.
3. Cook for about 20 minutes until nearly ready and the water has almost dried up.
4. Add onion, tomato, curry powder and coconut milk. Boil until vegetables are tender.

Remove from heat and serve with ugali.

Variations
  (a) Any type of vegetable could be used instead of spinach.
  (b) A cupful of groundnut paste could be mixed with coconut milk.
  (c) Onion and tomato could be fried first in salad oil before adding it to cooked vegetable.
  (d) Any other powder or spice could be used instead of the curry powder.

DRIED MUSHROOM AND GREENS

2 servings

Ingredients

1 cupful clean dried mushrooms	2 small sized onions
1 bunch green vegetables	1 cupful ghee or butter
1 cupful milk	Salt to taste
	Water as required

Method
1. Wash dried mushrooms, cover with water and cook slowly until tender.

2. Clean and wash vegetables. Boil a cupful of water with a little salt. Add vegetables and cook until tender, for about 10 minutes.
3. Chop onions and fry in 2 spoonfuls of ghee until well cooked.
4. Add mushroom and greens and cook well for about 5 minutes.
5. Add milk and the remaining ghee and also salt if more is required.
6. Cook for about 5 minutes and remove from the fire.

   Serve hot with ugali.

Variations
   (a) Dried mushrooms could be soaked for about 1 hour before cooking to lessen the cooking time.
   (b) Fresh edible mushrooms could also be mixed with green vegetables.

POUNDED MUSHROOMS

4 servings

Ingredients

4 cupfuls fresh cleaned and chopped mushrooms
4 cupfuls fresh milk
1 cupful ghee or butter
2 medium sized onions
Salt to taste
4 small sized tomatoes— optional

Method
1. Pound mushrooms in a mortar or mince in a meat mincer.
2. Chop onions and also tomatoes if liked.
3. Fry onions in 2 spoonfuls of ghee in a strong pan until brown. Add tomatoes if liked.
4. Add mushrooms into the onions and mix well cooking for about 5 minutes.
5. Add milk and reduce the fire. Simmer until well cooked for about 30 minutes.
6. Add salt and ghee and cook for another 10 minutes.
7. Remove from the fire and serve hot with ugali.

Variations
- (a) Sour milk could be used instead of fresh milk.
- (b) If milk is not enough, mushrooms could be cooked in water first until it is ready and then one cup of milk can be added towards the end of the cooking period.

SAVOURY PUMPKIN FRITTERS

4-6 servings

Ingredients

1 cupful cooked and mashed pumpkin
2 eggs
1 cupful flour
1 teaspoonful baking powder
Salt and pepper to taste
fat or oil for frying

Method
1. Heat oil in a clean pan until smoky hot.
2. Mix together all ingredients and shape the mixture as required.
3. Fry the mixture in hot oil about 5 minutes until crisp and brown.
4. Serve hot for 4-6 people.

Variations
- (a) The above could be turned into sweet fritters by adding a little cinnamon and 2 spoonfuls of sugar into the mixture before frying. When sweet fritters are served, place sliced lemon and sugar on top.
- (b) Sweet potatoes or plantain could be used in place of pumpkin.

SIMSIM (ROAST SESAME WITH GROUNDNUTS)

12 servings

Ingredients

2 cupfuls sesame
1 cupful groundnuts
2 teaspoonfuls salt

Method
1. Clean and soak the sesame in salty water for 1 hour. Rinse several times and drain well.
2. Roast in a dry heat (no fat or oil) in a strong pan over a slow fire or under the grill, turning very frequently all the time to prevent burning. Make sure that the sesame is dry and crisp but not burned.
3. Remove from the heat and spread on a tray to cool.
4. Clean groundnuts and wash them in a sieve. Drain well and sprinkle salt over them.
5. Roast in a dry heat as for the sesame above. When dry and crisp, remove from the heat and mix with sesame.

Serve in small dishes.

Variations
(a) Pulses such as green gram or cow peas could be used instead of groundnuts. If used they must be half-cooked in salty water first for about 30 minutes before roasting.
(b) Sugar could be added to taste instead of salt.

NOTE: This dish is not a main dish. It could be used as a snack or appetiser (hors d'oeuvre).

COW BLOOD COOKERY

Cow blood formed part of a special African diet, particularly among the pastoral people.

COW BLOOD COOKED IN SOUR MILK

4 servings

Ingredients
4 cupfuls fresh blood
4 cupfuls sour milk—2 days old
1 cupful ghee or butter
Salt to taste—optional

Method
1. Stir fresh blood and sieve to separate liquid from clot.
2. Mix milk and liquid blood and then pour in a pan.
3. Cook over slow fire, stirring to prevent burning for about 30 minutes.
4. Add ghee or butter and also salt if liked. The dish does not usually require salt due to sour milk.
5. Cover the pan and simmer for a further 10 minutes, stirring to prevent burning. The mixture should be thick like scrambled egg, but taste like cheese sauce.
6. Remove from the fire and serve with ugali, sweet potatoes or steamed plantain.

COW BLOOD COOKED IN FRESH MILK

2-3 servings

Ingredients
3 cupfuls cow blood
1 cupful fresh milk
½ cupful ghee or margarine
1 small sized onion—optional
Salt to taste

Method
1. Stir and separate liquid blood from the clot as in the sour milk cooking.
2. Chop onions into small pieces and put in a clean strong pan.
3. Add half of the ghee and fry until onions are brown.
4. Mix blood with milk and pour into the onions in the pan.
5. Cook over a slow fire stirring to prevent burning. Add more milk if the mixture becomes too thick.

6. Add the remaining half of ghee and also salt.
7. Cover the pan, reduce heat and simmer for about 15 minutes.
8. Remove from the fire and serve hot with ugali, bread, or boiled rice. This dish tastes like scrambled egg.

STUFFED MUTURA AND MAHU

10-12 servings

Ingredients

Mutura and mahu of a goat or a sheep.
(Selected soft cuts from all parts of the animal. The fatty meat which remained after heating and removing the oil from it. All the blood obtained from the slaughtered animal.)
1 cupful chopped onions
Salt and pepper to taste
A number of wooden skewers as required.

Method

1. Cut mutura in the middle in order to get 2 equal parts. Wash both parts and the 2 mahu to remove semi-digested chewed plants eaten by the animal. Put all 4 pieces of meat in a strainer to drain away water.
2. Chop meat into small pieces or mince if necessary and add onions, salt and pepper, and put in a pan.
3. Cook meat in its own juice which comes out when heated, turning frequently to prevent burning.
4. Cover the pan and cook for about 20 minutes, keep on turning to prevent burning.
5. Add the fatty meat from which oil had been drained away, and mix well. Make sure that salt and pepper are enough.
6. Remove meat from the fire add all the blood available and stuff or fill the 4 pieces of meat with the mixture until all is used up.
7. With wooden skewers join together both ends of each piece of mutura and also the open parts of mahu holding firmly to prevent the meat from falling off.
8. Roast or barbecue mutura and mahu very slowly over a low charcoal fire for about 2 hours, holding the meat with a bigger wooden skewer.

9. Prick the bags with a small wooden skewer to taste in order to make sure whether the meat is ready. When the blood changes into meat juices and it comes out with steam, the meat is ready.
10. Remove from the fire and serve together with barbecued liver and kidney.

Variations
   (a) Small intestines of a cow could also be used in the same way as mutura, and it is called mara. Those of a goat or a sheep, however, are too small to be stuffed. They are barbecued and eaten as they are.
   (b) Meat could be minced instead of chopped especially if they are the tougher cut of a cow's meat.
   (c) The above dish could be cooked in water instead of roasted but the flavour would not be as tasty as the roasted one.
   (d) Some people prefer to leave out onions and pepper. The preparation of this dish varies slightly from place to place.
   (e) Instead of cutting it into pieces, mutura could be stuffed whole.
   (f) Instead of using skewers, mutura's ends could be tied with banana fibres or any other string, before roasting.

N.B. This dish is extremely rich and satisfying so it does not require ugali or potatoes.

KAT AYIENYA (LUO), A SPECIAL SAUCE FOR DRIED MEAT OR FISH

6 servings

Ingredients
1 cupful ghee—usually home made
1½ cupfuls water
2 spoonfuls bala—salt—sesquicarbonate

Method
  1. Soak "bala" in 1 cupful of water and allow to stand for about 1 hour so that the sediments stay down.
  2. Drain bala water slowly so as to get 1 cupful of bala solution without pieces of bala or sediments. If the solution tastes strong, add more water to dilute it.

3. Warm ghee and let it become cold but still liquid.
4. Pour the bala water into ghee and the mixture will quickly turn white.
5. Make sure that the gravy of cooked meat or fish is cold. Add the prepared sauce to it and serve at once with ugali.

N.B. The colour of this sauce will not stay white when heated.

Variation

Bicarbonate of soda or magadi soda could be used instead of bala.

COOKERY OF SPECIAL INSECTS

Some special insects such as white ants, grasshoppers and locusts were a delicacy among some Africans. Each kind of these insects were caught by experts who used different methods. The insects were boiled in salty water, dried in the sun for preservation and then sold in market places, or kept for future meals.

FRIED WHITE ANTS

2 servings

Ingredients

1 cupful 1-2 day old white ants $\frac{1}{2}$ cupful water
Salt to taste   2 Spoonfuls ghee or butter

Method
1. Clean white ants by removing wings and stones or soil which might have been included.
2. Put insects in a pan and add water and salt.
3. Boil quickly for about 10 minutes until all water is evaporated.
4. Reduce heat and add ghee.
5. Cover the pot to allow ghee to soak in.
6. Remove from the fire and serve hot with ugali or steamed matoke.

FRIED GRASSHOPPERS OR LOCUSTS

4 servings

Ingredients

4 cupfuls 1-2 day old locusts or grasshoppers
2 cupfuls water
Salt to taste
1 cupful ghee or butter

Method
1. Remove wings and limbs from each insect.
2. Put insects in a strong pan and add salt and water.
3. Cook slowly for about 30 minutes or until soft.
4. Boil quickly till the water evaporates.
5. Reduce the heat and add half of the ghee.
6. Fry on a slow fire until insects become crisp.
7. Add the remaining ghee and cook for 5 minutes.
8. Remove from the fire and serve hot with ugali or matoke.

Variations
(a) A special type of ant known as onyoso in Luo could be used in place of white ants. These are seasonal insects which are only found during the rainy season in a certain time of the year.
(b) A special type of green grasshopper known in Luganda as senene or senesene in Luo which is a real delicacy in Kampala could be used in place of locusts or ordinary grasshoppers. These seasonal insects come in swarms and can be seen round the street lights at night. They come at a certain period of the year.

ASIAN RECIPES

TANDOORI CHICKEN

6 servings

Ingredients

1 roaster chicken	1 teaspoonful ginger powder
1 large-sized onion	or chopped fresh ginger
1 teaspoonful chilli powder	1½ teaspoonful coriander seeds
3 cloves garlic	1 teaspoonful paprika
2 spoonfuls lemon juice	A little yoghourt
1 teaspoonful cumin powder	A little oil or melted butter
	Salt to taste

Method

1. Clean and skin the chicken then prick it with a knife.
2. Mince the onion and garlic together, or chop finely.
3. Mix together onion, garlic, ginger, coriander, cumin, chilli and yoghourt then pass the whole lot through a mincer. Add half quantity lemon juice then rub mixture all over chicken.
4. Leave in a cool place from 4 hours to a whole day.
5. Put oil in a strong, non-sticking pan and heat. Fry chicken using moderate fire and turn it over from time to time until all parts are cooked. Turn up heat to make chicken brown and crisp.
6. Warm other half lemon juice and pour over chicken before serving.
7. Serve hot with chapatis, or Ceylon coconut bread, or Ceylon yellow rice.

Variations

(a) A simpler method is to rub over the chicken a mixture of salt, lemon juice, ½ teaspoonful chilli powder, 1 teaspoonful paprika and 2 cloves crushed garlic. Fry as above.

(b) A whole fish, such as tilapia, could be used instead of chicken. The fish must be brown and crisp when ready to eat.

(c) Instead of frying the chicken it could be roasted under a grill over charcoal fire—barbecue—or in oven. If cooked this way, basting with melted butter or oil should be done more frequently.

(d) Chicken could be cut into pieces before the mixture is rubbed in.

SHISH KEBAB BARBECUE

6 servings

Ingredients
Enough meat for 6—lean beef, mutton or veal
3 spoonfuls curry powder
2 spoonfuls curry paste
1 cupful yoghourt or curd
lemon juice from 1 lemon
A little fat

Method
1. Mix the curry powder with curry paste and moisten it with lemon juice.
2. Add yoghourt or curd to curry mixture.
3. Cut or scratch meat deeply in several places, put curry mixture into cuts and leave for 1 hour.
4. Cut meat into squares and leave for another hour.
5. Thread meat onto skewers and put over charcoal fire on a wire tray, or, under a grill.
6. Cook for about 10 minutes basting once or twice with little fat or dripping.
7. Remove from skewers and serve hot with chapati or Ceylon coconut bread—roti.

Variation
Put thin slices of fresh ginger-root or green peppers between pieces of meat before cooking.

CHICKEN PILAU

6 servings

Ingredients
1 roaster chicken
2 large onions
2 cupfuls rice
4 spoonfuls oil or fat
1 bay leaf
A few cloves
3 black cardamons or peppercorns
A little crushed garlic
4 spoonfuls shelled groundnuts or cashewnuts
Salt to taste

Method
1. Clean chicken and cut into small pieces. Boil the pieces of chicken together with salt, cloves, cardamons and garlic until nearly tender.
2. Wash rice and boil it in 4 cupfuls of water with bay leaf until nearly ready.
3. Remove pieces of chicken from its stock. Slice and fry onions in pan until golden brown.
4. Add pieces of chicken to onion and fry until brown.
5. Add cooked rice into mixture and also add chicken stock.
6. Roast nuts and add into mixture.
7. Cook over a slow heat for about 30 minutes until rice has absorbed most of chicken stock.

Serve hot with tomato salad and green chillies.

Variations
(a) Different kinds of peas or beans could be used in place of chicken if vegetarian dish is needed.
(b) Rice could be boiled in coconut milk first instead of water.
(c) The following could be added to chicken when frying: stoned raisins, 2 spoonfuls blanched almonds, 2 spoonfuls sliced and dried apricots, 2 spoonfuls ground cinnamon, ground cumin seeds, $\frac{1}{4}$ teaspoon each.

CURRIED LAMB OR MUTTON

6 servings

Ingredients

Lamb or mutton—enough for 6 people
2 spoonfuls dhania and jerra—geera—powder, mixed
½ spoonful mixed and ground cinnamon
½ spoonful cloves
1 spoonful tumeric
1 piece green ginger
6 small cloves garlic
8 medium-sized onions
2 spoonfuls tomato puree
6 medium-sized fresh tomatoes
4 spoonfuls ghee or butter
3 spoonfuls chutney
1 bunch spinach
A little oil
Curry powder, pepper and a little chilli to taste

Method
1. Clean meat and cut into small pieces.
2. Slice onions and tomatoes and chop garlic, ginger and spinach.
3. Fry onion and garlic in oil in a pan until golden brown.
4. Add meat and all other ingredients and cook slowly until meat absorbs the sauce.
5. Cover mixture with water and simmer until meat is tender, stirring from time to time to stop burning.

Serve hot with boiled rice or chapati.

FISH AND COCONUT CURRY

2 servings

Ingredients

1 large or 2 small whole fish —ngege
3 medium-sized onions
8 spoonfuls grated coconut
4 spoonfuls oil or ghee
4 spoonfuls tumeric
2 spoonfuls vinegar
3 chopped green chillies
Salt and dhania to taste

Method
1. Brown the onion in ghee or oil. Add tumeric, vinegar and salt and cook gently for 5 minutes.
2. Remove skin and bones from fish and add to mixture. Do not cook the fish flesh at this stage.

3. Add coconut to the sauce and cook slowly until soft.
4. Strain this sauce, removing bones and skin, and return it to pan.
5. Put fish flesh in the sauce and cook gently for about 15 minutes until soft.

Serve hot with white boiled rice, garnished with chopped dhania.

CEYLON YELLOW RICE

6 servings

Ingredients

2 cupfuls good quality rice
1 medium sized onion
1 teaspoonful ground cloves
1 teaspoonful cardamon
1 bayleaf
½ teaspoonful tumeric
4 cupfuls coconut milk
A little oil
2 spoonfuls butter
Salt to taste

Method

1. Clean and wash rice.
2. Slice onion and fry half of it with oil in a heavy pan together
   with bay leaf until brown.
3. Add rice and mix well with onion.
4. Add coconut milk and rest of the onions, salt, tumeric and cloves. Simmer gently for about 15 minutes until nearly ready.
5. Then add cardamon powder and cook for another 10 minutes until ready.

Serve hot with curried lamb or mutton.

ROTI (CEYLON COCONUT BREAD)

6 servings

Ingredients

2 cupfuls wheat flour
2 cupfuls desiccated coconut
A little butter or ghee
Salt to taste

Method
1. Roast flour gently in the oven or heat slightly in a pan.
2. Mix flour and coconut in a bowl and add a little boiling water to make a thick paste.
3. Form mixture into egg-sized balls and then flatten to size of a saucer.
4. Cook Roti in the same way as for chapati, see recipe.

Serve hot with Shish Kebab or curried fish or stew.

N.B. Rice flour, if obtainable, is the best for this dish.

CHAPATI

6 servings

Ingredients
1 cupful white flour
1 cupful wholemeal flour
1 spoonful oil
1 spoonful butter or ghee
Salt to taste

Method
1. Sift flour into a bowl and add salt and oil. Add enough cold water to mix flour into stiff dough. Knead well.
2. Cover with damp cloth and leave to stand for about 3 hours.
3. Knead well again and divide into egg size balls. Flatten each ball and roll out thinly into sizes of tea plates.
4. Wipe a non-stick frying pan, or a griddle, with a piece of paper greased with butter or ghee, then slowly heat the first chapati.
5. Cook on one side for about 1 minute, then turn over Press sides of chapati with wooden spoon until it puffs up. Remove chapati from pan or griddle, put on warm dish and butter one side.
6. Repeat this operation for every chapati, wiping pan or griddle with greased paper every time a new chapati is to be fried. Serve as soon as possible after cooking.

N.B. To keep them warm, pile them up wrapped in cloth or piece of aluminium foil and keep in warm oven, or, in non-stick frying pan covered with tight lid.

SAMOSAS

6 servings

Ingredients

PASTRY
1 cupful plain flour
2 teaspoonfuls oil
½ teaspoonful lemon juice
Salt to taste

PASTE FOR SEALING
2 spoonfuls plain flour

FILLING
Minced meat—enough for 6 people
4 medium sized onions
1 red chilli
1 green chilli
½ teaspoonful crushed ginger
½ teaspoonful powdered cloves
½ teaspoonful powdered cinnamon
1 teaspoonful lemon juice
1 bunch dhania
A little oil
Salt to taste

Method for Filling
1. Put minced meat, ginger, chopped red and green chillies and salt into a sauce-pan and cook for 15 minutes.
2. Add chopped onions and dhania, powdered cloves and cinnamon and lemon juice.
3. Cook for a while, remove from heat and allow to cool.

Method for Pastry
1. Sift flour into a bowl and add salt and oil. Add lemon juice and enough cold water to make a stiff dough. Knead well.
2. Divide the mixture into size of small balls. Flatten three balls at a time and roll them out to size of saucers.
3. Brush the upper parts of two with a mixture of oil and flour. Place the third as top layer on top of the other two and roll all three together into ¼ inch thickness.
4. Cook over a hot plate or griddle for about 2 minutes on each side.
5. Remove from heat and peel the three rounds apart carefully. Cut them into strips of 3 inches wide. Take one strip and fill it with minced meat mixture—filling—and fold to make a 3-cornered case.
6. Make the sealing paste with flour and water and seal the

ends of all cases.
7. Fry in deep hot oil until golden brown. Drain in absorbent paper and serve hot.

Variations
(a) Yoghourt could be mixed with the pastry instead of water especially when vegetable filling is used in place of meat.
(b) Vegetables, such as peas and potatoes could be used for filling instead of minced meat.
(c) Baking powder could be added to flour—$\frac{1}{2}$ teaspoonful to 1 cupful flour.

CURRY PASTE OR CURRY SAUCE

*Servings**

Ingredients

1 small finely chopped or crushed onion
1 clove crushed garlic
1 piece fresh crushed ginger
1 spoonful mixed spices
A few crushed green chillies
2 small tomatoes
1 spoonful tomato puree
A little oil or dripping

Method
1. Fry chopped onion in oil until golden brown.
2. Add all other ingredients. Simmer for about 10 minutes.
3. Remove from heat, cool and serve as required.

N.B. Ready made curry paste or curry sauce can be bought from Asian shops but it is cheaper to prepare at home.

*The above sauce is usually kept in a bottle and used as required (see page 87 where only 2 spoonfuls are required for 6 servings).

EUROPEAN RECIPES

APPETIZERS

AVOCADO PEARS WITH HARD BOILED EGG

6 servings

Ingredients
3 avocado pears—allow ½ per person
1 hard-boiled egg
1 ripe tomato
A little lemon juice
1 small lettuce

Method
1. Cut soft avocado in half lengthways and remove the stone.
2. Cover the flesh with lemon juice to keep it from going brown.
3. Shred lettuce, slice egg and tomato.
4. Mix the ingredients together and fill avocado centre with the mixture.
5. Serve, placing avocado and its contents in neat small dishes as first course or hors d'oeuvre, or as liked.

AVOCADO PEAR WITH CHOPPED PRAWNS

6 servings

Ingredients

Half avacado pear per person	¼ cup diced pineapple
1 sweet pepper—diced	A little lemon juice
	1 Cupful cooked and chopped prawns

Method
1. Squeeze lemon juice over flesh.
2. Fill the centre with a mixture of the above ingredients.
3. Serve as first course or hors d'oeuvre or as required.

AVOCADO PEARS WITH OIL AND VINEGAR

6 servings

Ingredients

3 avocado pears	Vinegar to taste
2 spoonfuls good salad oil	Salt and pepper to taste

Method
1. Remove the pulp neatly from avocado cut in half lengthways.
2. Mix the pulp with oil, vinegar and season.
3. Return into the centre of avocado.
4. Serve as hors d'oeuvre, or as required.

AVOCADO PEARS WITH FISH

6 servings

Ingredients

3 avocado pears	1 medium sized tomato
1 cupful boiled chopped flesh of fish	Mayonnaise sauce to taste

Method
1. Cut avocado in half lengthways and remove the stone.
2. Fill the centre with a mixture of the above ingredients.
3. Serve as required.

AVOCADO PEARS WITH CHICKEN

6 servings

Ingredients

1 cupful diced cooked chicken flesh
3 avocado pears
1 cleaned lettuce
A little lemon juice

Method
1. Remove the pulp carefully and dice neatly into cubes.
2. Toss in lemon juice and add to diced chicken.
3. Mix well and pile on a bed of shredded lettuce in a dish.
4. Serve as required.

SOUPS

VEGETABLE SOUP

6 servings

Ingredients

3 medium sized potatoes
1 medium sized carrot
½ medium sized turnip
1 leek
1 spoonful margarine
2 spoonfuls flour
1 cupful milk
5 cupfuls boiling water
Salt and pepper to taste

Method
1. Clean vegetables then dice or shred in small pieces.
2. Melt the margarine in a soup pan and put in all vegetables.
3. Keep turning them until they absorb the margarine.
4. Pour on boiling water and add seasoning. Skim if necessary and simmer gently for about 1 hour until tender.
5. Mix flour with milk, stir into soup and cook for about 10 minutes.
Serve hot.

Variation
Any other type of root vegetables could be used.

CHICKEN SOUP

6 servings

Ingredients
1 medium sized boiler chicken
4 spoonfuls rice
2 leeks
8 cupfuls water
1 cupful milk
A little parsley
Salt and pepper to taste

Method
1. Clean and wash chicken. Put water into a soup pan and put chicken into it.
2. Simmer for 4-5 hours then remove chicken. Strain soup and return to the pot.
3. Wash and clean rice then add to soup. Cook slowly for about 30 minutes until rice is cooked. Add chopped leeks to soup.
4. Just before serving add finely chopped parsley and milk.

Serve hot.

Variation
Meat bones could be used instead of chicken and barley could replace the rice.

CREAM OF TOMATO SOUP

6 servings

Ingredients

6 medium sized ripe tomatoes	1 cupful stock or water
2 medium sized onions	A little bacon rind
2 spoonfuls corn flour	A pinch of sugar
1 cupful milk	Salt and pepper to taste

Method

1. Put bacon rind into a soup pot and add sliced onions once the rind is hot.
2. Slice tomatoes finely and add to onions when they are brown. Keep stirring until fat is absorbed.
3. Stew gently for about 1 hour with pot covered. Then add stock or water and simmer for a further $\frac{1}{2}$ hour. Strain and return to pot.
4. Mix milk and flour and add to soup to thicken. Add sugar before serving.

Serve hot.

GROUNDNUT SOUP

6 servings

Ingredients

2 cupfuls skinned and minced groundnuts	1 stick celery
	3 cupfuls milk
3 cupfuls white stock or water	1 spoonful butter
	2 spoonfuls flour
1 medium sized onion	2 spoonfuls cream

Method

1. Put into the pan groundnuts, chopped onion and celery with water or white stock. Simmer for 1 hour and rub through a sieve.
2. Melt butter and mix with flour then cook slightly for about 5 minutes and add to the soup. Add seasoning.
3. Bring to boil, stirring all the time, then add milk.
4. Boil again and just before serving add cream.

Serve hot.

MAIN DISHES

ROAST BEEF

4 servings

Ingredients

Ribs of beef or sirloin enough for 4 people
1 cupful or 8 spoonfuls oil or fat
4 cupfuls water
1 spoonful flour
Salt and pepper to taste

Method
1. Wipe and trim meat and place in baking tin. Pour over top of meat the oil or fat and place in very hot oven.
2. Leave for 10-15 minutes until outside of meat is sealed. Reduce heat and allow to cook until tender. Time allowance is 20 minutes to each 500 grams. Baste frequently with hot oil or fat every 10-15 minutes.
3. Remove meat and keep hot.
4. Pour most of hot oil from baking tin, leaving only a little sediment. Add flour and seasoning to sediment and stir well.
5. Add water and again stir well, then boil to make gravy to serve with meat.

Served usually with roast potatoes and Yorkshire Pudding.

Variations
Other meats could be used instead of beef.

ROAST POTATOES

Ingredients
2 Medium sized potatoes per person

Method
1. Peel and wash potatoes, then dry with cloth.
2. Place potatoes around meat in baking tin and baste frequently.
3. Keep turning until tender.

   Serve with roast meat.

ROAST CHICKEN

6 servings

Ingredients
1 medium sized roaster chicken   1 cupful water
2 cupfuls oil or fat   Salt and pepper to taste
2 spoonfuls flour

Method
1. Clean and wash chicken then dry with cloth. Put in baking pan and dredge with flour.
2. Pour oil or fat over chicken and bake, basting frequently, every 10-15 minutes for about 30 minutes, or until tender. Lift out the bird on to a hot dish and keep hot.
3. Pour off oil from pan, leaving only a little.
4. Add flour and seasoning, then mix with water. Simmer for about 10 minutes.
5. Strain gravy and serve with chicken and Parsley stuffing.

Variations
Any other bird such as duck, pigeon, turkey or guinea-fowl could be used instead of chicken.

N.B. Accompaniment of turkey is Chestnut stuffing, and for duck or goose use sage and onion stuffing. (See recipes.)

POT ROAST

4 servings

Ingredients
Beef or mutton for roasting—enough for 4 people
4 spoonfuls ghee or oil
1 spoonful flour
½ cupful water or soup stock
Salt and pepper to taste

Method
1. Wipe and trim meat then tie with fine string into shape.
2. Melt ghee or oil in strong stewing pan or earthenware pot.
3. Heat oil smoking hot, add meat and brown thoroughly on all sides.
4. Cover and draw pot to side of stove and cook slowly for about 1½ hours until tender, basting with oil frequently.
5. Lift from pot but keep hot.
6. Make gravy with flour, water or stock and seasoning, as for roast beef, and serve.

MUSHROOM CHICKEN AND RICE CASSEROLE

6 servings

Ingredients
1 boiled chicken—not overcooked
2 cupfuls cooked rice
1 cupful shelled and roasted groundnuts
¾ cupful chopped green peppers
1 cupful cleaned and chopped mushrooms
1 cupful mushroom powdered soup—sold in packets
4 cupfuls chicken stock
2 spoonfuls butter
1 small sized chopped onion
2 cupfuls potato crisps
Salt and pepper to taste

Method
1. Remove chicken from bones, leaving only neat bones. Chop the flesh and longer bones into big pieces. Crush the nuts roughly.
2. Take 2 cupfuls of chicken stock and make mushroom soup with it. Soup powder is ordinary Knorr or Maggi packet of creamed mushroom soup. The soup should be very thick when ready.

3. Grease a casserole dish with some of the measured butter.
4. Put pieces of chicken in a big bowl and then add all other ingredients together into the chicken except the potato crisps.
5. At the last moment crumble most of the crisps and add to the mixture, and then turn the whole lot into the greased casserole.
6. Scatter the remaining crisps and pieces of butter on top of the mixture. Make sure that the top is covered by crisps.
7. Bake in the oven at 375°F for about ¾ hour.

Serve hot as a complete meal.

Variations
(a) Almonds could be used in place of groundnuts but they should be blanched and chopped.
(b) A larger quantity of rice could be added to increase the quantity of meal.

N.B. This dish could be prepared well in advance and kept in the refrigerator leaving out the crisps for the last moment.

KEBAB BARBECUE

4 servings
Ingredients as for Meat Barbecue recipe, plus a little butter or margarine and a little lemon juice.

Method
1. Choose the meat, then cut up into one inch squares. Season and thread on to skewers.
2. Grill over a charcoal fire or low, red fire, turning the skewer occasionally and brushing meat with butter or margarine and with a little lemon juice.
3. Cook until all parts are done then serve with a suitable sauce, and roast potatoes in their jackets.

Variations for Kebab mixtures:
(a) Steak, tomato and mushroom.
(b) Sausages, onions and tomatoes.
(c) Veal, steak and pineapple

(d) Ham squares, banana and pineapple
(e) Kidney and bacon.
   Or, any variety of the above.

PORK CHOP BARBECUE

4 servings

Ingredients

4 pork chops	4 spoonfuls vinegar
4 spoonfuls chopped pineapple	1 teaspoonful mustard
2 teaspoonfuls worcester sauce	2 spoonfuls tomato juice
1 spoonful butter	2 teaspoonfuls brown sugar
A little melted lard	Salt and pepper to taste

Method
1. Brush the chops all over with a little melted lard.
2. Put them over a wire tray on top of charcoal stove or under pre-heated grill. Heat for few minutes on each side then add seasoning.
3. Melt butter in a small pan and add rest of ingredients above. Simmer for about 2 minutes. Turn grill to low heat then baste chops with sauce.
4. Turn chops two or three times continuing to baste with sauce.
5. Cook until ready—about 20 minutes.

Serve hot with any remaining sauce, and fried potatoes in their jackets and fresh vegetable salad.

FRIED STEAK AND ONIONS

2 servings

Ingredients

Tender piece of steak enough for 2 people	1 spoonful fat or oil
	½ cupful water
1 medium sized onion	Salt and pepper to taste

Method
1. Wipe, trim slice thickly, then beat the steak and add in seasoning.

2. Slice onions in rings and fry in frying-pan until brown.
3. Make oil smoking hot and fry steak quickly on both sides, then cook slowly for 10-15 minutes until tender.
4. Remove and place on a hot dish with the onions.
5. Pour water into the pan, boil, add seasoning and then serve with steak, and chipped English potatoes.

FRIED CHICKEN IN BREADCRUMBS

6 servings

Ingredients
1 roaster chicken	2 spoonfuls vinegar
1 egg	Breadcrumbs as required
2 spoonfuls butter	Salt and pepper to taste
4 spoonfuls salad oil	

Method
1. Cut chicken into small joints and lay on plate. Cover with oil and vinegar and sprinkle with salt and pepper. Stand for 3 hours.
2. Beat egg and brush pieces of chicken with beaten egg and dip each piece in breadcrumbs.
3. Melt butter, brush over breadcrumbs and again dip into breadcrumbs.
4. Fry pieces of chicken slowly in remaining butter in a frying-pan for about 20 minutes until tender.

Serve hot and at once, with roast or fried English potatoes

FRIED FISH

2 servings

Ingredients
1 whole fish	Flour or breadcrumbs as required
2 eggs	
2 spoonfuls fat or oil	Salt and pepper to taste

Method
1. Remove bones from fish, wash and dry in a cloth.
2. Cut into fillets and dry then sprinkle with salt and pepper.

3. Dip into beaten egg. Roll in breadcrumbs or flour.
4. Fry in smoking hot oil or fat to a golden brown. Turn and fry on other side.
5. Cook thoroughly for about 15 minutes, drain off oil and Serve hot at once with chipped English potatoes.

Variations
Fillets of fish could be dipped into a butter made of a little flour, salt and water before frying instead of in the egg.

MAYONNAISE SAUCE
(to accompany grilled or fried fish)

6 servings

Ingredients

3 egg yolks
1 cupful salad oil
½ teaspoonful salt

½ teaspoonful dry mustard
½ teaspoonful sugar
2 spoonfuls lemon juice or lime juice

Method
1. Put egg yolks, salt and sugar into a bowl. Blend in the oil, slowly, beating with an egg beater.
2. Add lemon or lime juice, and blend thoroughly.
3. Taste and add more seasoning if desired.

FRIED BACON AND EGGS

2 servings

Ingredients
2 slices bacon   2 eggs

Method
1. Remove bacon rind and some of the fat and place in clean frying pan using low heat.
2. Fry bacon slightly underdone and then remove and keep hot.

3. Heat remaining fat in pan until slightly smoking. Break the eggs gently into a cup then place gently into pan. Reduce heat and baste continuously keeping the yolks as round as possible. Cook until slighly set.
4. Put bacon back in pan briefly but do not overcook.
5. Drain eggs from fat, place on top of bacon and serve hot.

Variations
(a) Fry a slice of bread on both sides until brown, in remaining fat then serve eggs and bacon on top.
(b) Boil bacon in a cupful of water for about 5 minutes before frying, if it is salty. Pour away remaining water.

FRIED SAUSAGES AND BACON

4 servings

Ingredients
4 sausages   Very little fat or oil
4 slices bacon

Method
1. Heat oil quickly in a frying pan and then reduce heat.
2. Fry bacon gently taking care not to dry it out. Remove bacon from pan and keep hot.
3. Prick sausages with a fork and fry slowly until all parts are cooked and nicely brown.
4. Put in a hot dish with bacon and serve at once.

Variations
(a) Kidney, or liver, could be used instead of sausages.
(b) Both bacon and sausages have fat in them so extra fat or oil is sometimes not necessary.

FRIED CHOPS AND LIVER

2 Servings

Ingredients
Loin or neck chops, enough for 2 people   1 spoonful flour
Liver—enough for 2 people   1 cupful water
1 small sized onion   1 spoonful fat or oil
   Salt and pepper to taste.

Method
1. Trim the chops, wipe carefully, add seasoning and beat until softened.
2. Wash and dry liver, add seasoning and cut into thick slices.
3. Heat oil in a frying pan and fry sliced onion until brown.
4. Remove onion and keep hot.
5. Fry liver quickly for about 5 minutes until cooked. Remove from heat and keep hot.
6. Fry chop quickly on both sides and then let it cook slowly for about 30 minutes until tender. Remove from the heat, place with the liver and garnish with the onions.
7. Put flour in the pan and brown but do not burn. Add water and seasoning and boil slowly until tasty.
8. Serve with liver, chops and chipped English potatoes.

MEAT BALLS

2 servings

Ingredients
2 cupfuls minced meat
2 spoonfuls chopped onion
4 Spoonfuls flour
$\frac{1}{4}$ cupful oil or fat
Salt and pepper to taste

Method
1. Mix all ingredients together except oil or fat and use only 2 spoonfuls of the flour.
2. Form mixture into even sized balls using remainder of flour to prevent mixture from sticking.
3. Melt oil or fat in baking tray and place balls of meat on tray. Bake in oven using moderate heat. Baste occasionally until cooked—about 30 minutes.
Best served hot, with gravy and mashed potatoes.

FRIED MEAT BALLS

4 servings

Ingredients
2 thick slices bread	2 eggs
Uncooked minced beef or lamb enough for 4	2 spoonfuls crisp breadcrumbs
	Salt and pepper to taste
1 medium sized grated or minced onion	Fat or oil for frying
	4-6 spoonfuls warm milk or tomato juice
Mixed herbs—optional	

Method
1. Remove the crusts from the bread and soak break in milk or tomato juice.
2. Beat bread until smooth and add minced meat, onions, one egg, salt and pepper and herbs.
3. Form the mixture into a small ball.
4. Roll in the remaining beaten egg and crisp breadcrumbs.
5. Heat oil or fat in a frying pan and fry meat balls steadily in the fat on low fire until golden brown—for about 10 minutes.
   Serve hot.

SCOTCH EGGS

2 servings

Ingredients
Sausage meat from 4 sausages or enough for 2 people	1 egg
	2 cupfuls oil
2 hard-boiled eggs	Breadcrumbs

Method
1. Shell the hard-boiled eggs. Make sure they are cold then cover them with sausage meat, about ¼ inch thickness all over.
2. Coat sausage meat with beaten egg then dip in breadcrumbs.
3. Heat the oil until smoking hot then deep-fry the sausage-egg for about 5 minutes until ready.
4. Cut the sausage-eggs in two halves and serve hot or cold with mashed potatoes and a suitable sauce.

STUFFED EGG PLANT

4 servings

Ingredients
- 2 large sized egg plants
- 2 spoonfuls peanut butter or margarine
- 1 medium sized chopped onion
- 1 cupful cooked minced beef or lamb
- 2 medium sized tomatoes
- 1 spoonful margarine or butter
- 2 spoonfuls dried breadcrumbs
- Salt to taste

Method
1. Wash egg plant and cut into half.
2. Scoop out pulp, leaving a thin shell.
3. Dice pulp and cook in fat or peanut butter over a low fire until soft.
4. Add onion and mix with the rest of ingredients except 1 spoonful margarine and breadcrumbs.
5. Fill the egg plant shell with the mixture and sprinkle with crumbs.
6. Put margarine on top and brown in a hot oven for about 15 minutes or under the grill for about 5 minutes.

Serve hot with mashed potatoes.

MINCED LAMB PIE

4-6 servings

Ingredients
- Minced lamb enough for 4-6 people
- 2 medium sized chopped onions
- 2 thick slices of bread
- 1½ cupfuls milk
- 2 small eggs
- 1 spoonful sugar
- 2 spoonfuls curry powder
- 1 teaspoonful salt
- 2 spoonfuls lemon juice or table vinegar
- 2 spoonfuls fat or butter

Method
1. Heat fat in a pan, add onions and cook until brown and soft.
2. And curry powder, salt, sugar and lemon juice or vinegar and mix thoroughly.
3. Soak slices of bread in the milk for about 15 minutes.

4. Remove bread from milk and beat till very soft.
5. Add bread to the fried onion mixture together with lamb and one of the eggs.
6. Pour into a well greased pie dish.
7. Beat the second egg and add the milk drained from the bread — about ¾ cup.
8. Bake in the middle of a moderately hot oven for about 30 minutes.
9. Reduce the heat and cook for a further 30 minutes.

Serve hot as required with mashed potatoes.

CURRIED MUTTON

2 servings

Ingredients

Neck of mutton, or mutton chops—enough for 2 people
1 chopped apple
1 onion
1 spoonful wheat flour
1 spoonful sultanas
Stock or water to cover the meat
Curry powder, sugar, salt, chutney and tomatoes to taste

Method
1. Wipe, trim and cut mutton into suitable pieces for serving.
2. Add the stock or water to the meat in a boiler and simmer for about 2 hours until tender. Remove all fat.
3. Slice and fry onion in a little oil until brown.
4. Mix curry powder and flour until it is a smooth mixture.
5. Add mixture to the meat one hour before serving.
6. Add chopped apples, sultanas, sugar, salt, chutney and tomatoes ½ hour before serving.

Serve with boiled rice.

Variation
(a) Chicken could be used instead of mutton.

MINCED MEAT AND ONIONS

2 servings

Ingredients

Minced meat—enough for two people
1 small sized onion
1 spoonful wheat flour
1 spoonful fat or oil
1 cupful water
Salt and pepper to taste

Method
1. Heat the fat until smoking hot and add minced meat and chopped onion.
2. Fry until brown then add flour and water. Bring to the boil and add seasoning.
3. Simmer gently for about 1 hour until tender.

Serve hot with mashed English potatoes.

STEWED CHICKEN

6 servings

Ingredients

1 medium sized boiler chicken
2 spoonfuls butter or ghee
12 small mushrooms
2 slices ham
1 spoonful flour
Enough stock or water to cover
Salt and pepper to taste

Method
1. Clean chicken and cut into pieces. Dry and fry quickly in butter or ghee and add the ham.
2. Add stock or water and the seasoning and bring to boiling point.
3. Skin mushrooms, wash and add to chicken.
4. Simmer for about 1 hour, until tender, then remove both chicken and mushrooms.
5. Thicken gravy with flour, strain, then pour over the chicken in a dish.
6. Garnish with mushrooms and serve.

Variations

Any other bird, such as duck or pigeon could be cooked in this way.

STEWED FISH

4 servings

Ingredients

Fish—enough for 4 people
1 cupful water
1 coconut
1 cupful coconut milk
1 spoonful butter
Salt and pepper to taste

Method
1. Wash the fish, then fillet it and put it aside in cold salted water.
2. Put fish bones and skin in a saucepan.
3. Add milk from the coconut, water and the rest of the coconut grated.
4. Boil slowly for 2 hours then strain away bones and skin.
5. Put fish into remaining liquid and add seasoning. Simmer for 15 minutes or until tender.
6. Add butter and serve hot.

Variation

When boiling bones and skin, add 2 bay leaves, 3 peppercorns and 3 cloves for a tastier dish.

ENGLISH STEW

2 servings

Ingredients

Beef—enough for 2 people
1 spoonful Fat or oil
1 spoonful wheat flour
1 small onion
Salt and pepper to taste

Method
1. Wipe, trim and cut beef into small pieces.
2. Heat fat in a strong pan until smoking hot. Fry onion, then lift out. Fry meat until brown on both sides.
3. Add hot water to cover the meat, then add onion and seasoning and simmer gently for about 2 hours until tender.
4. Blend flour with a little water until smooth and add to meat. Simmer for 10 more minutes.

Serve hot with boiled English potatoes.

IRISH STEW

2 servings

Ingredients
Mutton—enough for 2 people
2 medium sized potatoes
1 large sized onion
Salt and a little pepper to taste

Method
1. Wipe, trim and cut mutton into small pieces.
2. Put in a clean, strong pan and cover with hot water. Add salt then bring to the boil. Skim well.
3. Skin onions and slice into rings. Add onions to meat and simmer for 2 hours.
4. Wash and peel potatoes, slice one and halve the other. Add sliced potato to meat and also add salt and pepper.
5. Simmer until tender then add the halved potatoes just $\frac{1}{2}$ hour before serving. Simmer until potatoes are soft and serve.

Variation
(a) $\frac{1}{2}$ cup of milk could be added at the same time when halved potatoes go in.

DUTCH STEW

4 servings

Shoulder of mutton—enough for 4 people
1 Spoonful fat or oil
1 small sized cabbage
1 small sized finely chopped onion
4 medium sized potatoes
Salt and pepper to taste

Method
1. Wipe mutton but do not cut.
2. Heat the oil and put in mutton with finely chopped onions.
3. Fry quickly until slightly brown.
4. Clean cabbage and cut into four. Peel and slice potatoes.
5. Put potatoes and cabbage in some water, then lift both and place them over the mutton without draining.
6. Add seasoning, cover the pan and simmer for about 2 hours until meat is tender.

7. Dish up neatly, mutton in centre, cabbage on top and potatoes around.

Serve with a liquid sauce or gravy.

Variation
(a) Use beef instead of mutton but add onion, liver and bacon to the meat one hour before serving.

BOILED BEEF AND CARROTS

4 servings

Ingredients

Beef—enough for 4 people
1 small sized turnip
2 large sized carrots
1 small sized onion
Water to cover the meat
Salt and pepper to taste

Method
1. Wipe and trim the meat.
2. Put water into a strong pan with salt, bring to boil and put in meat. Boil for about 5 minutes to seal outside of meat.
3. Wash and peel vegetables and cut into neat blocks. Add to meat and reduce heat.
4. Simmer for about 2 hours until meat is tender.
5. Serve in a dish with meat in the middle, vegetables around it, gravy all over it.

Variation
Mutton or other type of meat could be used instead of beef.

BOILED CHICKEN

6 servings

Ingredients

1 medium sized boiler chicken
1 medium sized onion
1 medium sized carrot
1 medium sized turnip
1 bay leaf
A little parsley
Enough water to cover meat
Salt to taste

Method
1. Clean and wash chicken and cover it with cloth.
2. Boil water, add salt and chopped vegetables.
3. Place chicken in boiling water and add bay leaf and reduce heat.
4. Simmer gently for about 1½ hours until tender.
5. Remove from pot and place on dish. Garnish with parsley.

Serve with a white sauce, and boiled English potatoes.

Variation
Any bird such as guinea fowl, or pigeon could be used instead of chicken.

GRILLED FISH WITH ORANGE BUTTER

4 servings

Ingredients
4 ngege—lake fish
4 spoonfuls butter or margarine
2 whole oranges cut into slices
Grated rind of ½ orange
Juice of 1 orange

Method
1. Clean fish, wash and dry.
2. Fry onion in half of the butter and add orange rind and juice.
3. Melt the remaining butter and brush fish with it.
4. Grill fish until nearly ready on both sides. The time required is about 10 minutes depending on the type of fish.
5. Add orange pieces and reheat.

Serve hot with orange butter poured over.

BAKED FISH (A)

2 servings

Ingredients
1 whole fish
3 spoonfuls butter
Salt and pepper to taste

Method
1. Clean fish well, dry and sprinkle with salt and pepper.
2. Place fish in baking dish or casserole and put butter on top.
3. Bake in oven for about 30 minutes until tender.

Serve at once in its own juice with mashed potatoes.

BAKED FISH (B)

2 servings

Ingredients
4 pieces fish fillets
1 small sized onion
2 small sized tomatoes
1 spoonful butter
Salt and pepper to taste

Method
1. Place fillets of fish in a greased baking dish.
2. Brush with melted butter and then sprinkle salt and pepper over them.
3. Slice onion and fry with a little butter until tender.
4. Spread onion over fish together with sliced tomatoes.
5. Bake all in a moderate oven for about 15 minutes until fish is tender.

Serve hot with boiled or mashed potatoes.

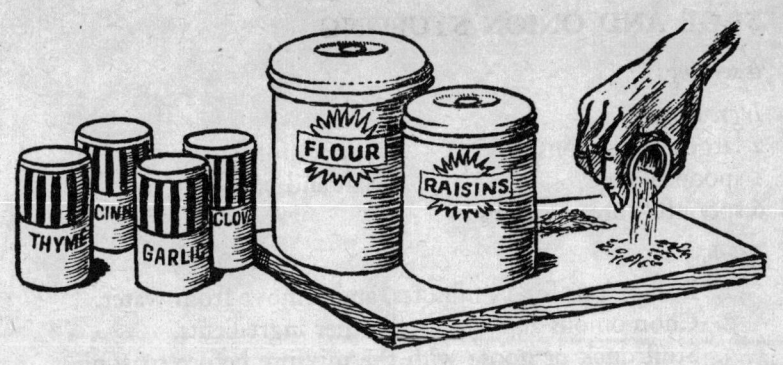

STUFFINGS

CHESTNUT STUFFING

6 servings

Ingredients
4 cupfuls chestnuts
1 spoonful melted butter
1 cupful stock or water
Salt and pepper to taste

Method
1. Split chestnut skins and bake for 20 minutes.
2. Remove outer and inner skins, put in a stewing pan and add just enough stock or water to cover.
3. Simmer slowly till tender then rub through a sieve.
4. Add melted butter, sugar, salt and pepper.
5. Stuff the bird with this mixture before roasting.

Variations
(a) Add 1 cupful breadcrumbs, 2 spoonfuls chopped parsley and 1 spoonful cream or milk to the above mixture.
(b) Add 2 cupfuls of sausage meat, well cooked to the above mixture.
(c) Use roasted groundnuts paste instead of chestnuts—groundnut stuffing.

SAGE AND ONION STUFFING

6 servings

Ingredients
2 large sized onions
1 spoonful sage
6 spoonfuls breadcrumbs
2 spoonfuls butter
Salt and pepper to taste

Method
1. Boil onions for 15 minutes, and remove from water.
2. Chop onions and add to all other ingredients.
3. Stuff duck or goose with the mixture before roasting.
4. When the duck or goose is ready, remove the stuffing and serve hot with roasted bird and gravy.

PARSLEY STUFFING

6 servings

Ingredients
1 cupful breadcrumbs or squeezed and dried soaked bread
2 spoonfuls chopped meat fat—suet—or melted fat
2 spoonfuls chopped parsley
1 grated rind of lemon
$\frac{1}{2}$ teaspoonful mixed herbs
1 beaten egg or a little milk
Salt and pepper to taste

Method
1. Mix all the ingredients together in a bowl.
2. Stuff the chicken with the mixture before baking. Fill the hollow part inside the chicken with the mixture and roast with the mixture in it.
3. When the roast chicken is ready, remove the stuffing and serve hot with chicken and gravy.

YORKSHIRE PUDDING

4 servings

Ingredients
8 spoonfuls flour
1 cupful milk
2 eggs
4 spoonfuls or 1 cupful fat or oil
$\frac{1}{4}$ spoonful salt

STUFFINGS

CHESTNUT STUFFING

6 servings

Ingredients
4 cupfuls chestnuts
1 spoonful melted butter
1 cupful stock or water
Salt and pepper to taste

Method
1. Split chestnut skins and bake for 20 minutes.
2. Remove outer and inner skins, put in a stewing pan and add just enough stock or water to cover.
3. Simmer slowly till tender then rub through a sieve.
4. Add melted butter, sugar, salt and pepper.
5. Stuff the bird with this mixture before roasting.

Variations
(a) Add 1 cupful breadcrumbs, 2 spoonfuls chopped parsley and 1 spoonful cream or milk to the above mixture.
(b) Add 2 cupfuls of sausage meat, well cooked to the above mixture.
(c) Use roasted groundnuts paste instead of chestnuts—groundnut stuffing.

SAGE AND ONION STUFFING

6 servings

Ingredients
2 large sized onions
1 spoonful sage
6 spoonfuls breadcrumbs
2 spoonfuls butter
Salt and pepper to taste

Method
1. Boil onions for 15 minutes, and remove from water.
2. Chop onions and add to all other ingredients.
3. Stuff duck or goose with the mixture before roasting.
4. When the duck or goose is ready, remove the stuffing and serve hot with roasted bird and gravy.

PARSLEY STUFFING

6 servings

Ingredients
1 cupful breadcrumbs or squeezed and dried soaked bread
2 spoonfuls chopped meat fat—suet—or melted fat
2 spoonfuls chopped parsley
1 grated rind of lemon
½ teaspoonful mixed herbs
1 beaten egg or a little milk
Salt and pepper to taste

Method
1. Mix all the ingredients together in a bowl.
2. Stuff the chicken with the mixture before baking. Fill the hollow part inside the chicken with the mixture and roast with the mixture in it.
3. When the roast chicken is ready, remove the stuffing and serve hot with chicken and gravy.

YORKSHIRE PUDDING

4 servings

Ingredients
8 spoonfuls flour
1 cupful milk
2 eggs
4 spoonfuls or 1 cupful fat or oil
¼ spoonful salt

Method
1. Put flour and salt in a bowl.
2. Make a hole in the flour centre. Break eggs and put into the hole together with some milk.
3. Stir with a wooden spoon gradually until all the flour is mixed, adding more of the remaining milk as required, until the mixture is like thick cream.
4. Beat hard for 10 minutes and then add the remaining milk gently.
5. Leave to stand in a cool place for 1 hour.
6. Heat the dripping or oil in a baking tin.
7. Pour the mixture in the oil and cook in a very hot oven for about 20 minutes or until the mixture is well risen, brown and crisp on the outside.
8. Cut into squares and serve around roast beef in a dish.

DISHES FROM LEFTOVERS

COTTAGE PIE—OR SHEPHERD'S PIE

2 servings

Ingredients

Cold, cooked meat, enough for 2 people
4 potatoes
1 spoonful margarine
¼ cupful milk
1 small sized onion
1 spoonful flour
1 spoonful oil or fat
1 cupful stock
Salt and pepper to taste

Method
1. Peel, wash and boil potatoes. Then mash. Mix them with margarine, milk, seasoning.
2. Cut meat and pass pieces through a mincer.
3. Heat oil or fat, then cook chopped onion until golden brown, add flour, a little water and more seasoning and stir.
4. Add meat to the mixture and mix well.
5. Pour mixture into a greased pie dish, then pile mashed potatoes on top of it. Brush over with a little milk.
6. Put in hot oven or under a grill for about 20 minutes.
7. When top of potatoes is golden brown remove and serve very hot.

Variation
Any type of meat could be used, even minced chicken.

RISSOLES

2 servings

Ingredients

Cold cooked meat—enough for 2 people
1 egg
A little breadcrumbs
2 cooked and mashed potatoes
1 spoonful flour
½ cupful soup stock
1 small sized onion
2 cupfuls oil or fat
Salt and pepper to taste

Method
1. Prepare meat by cutting it and passing through a mincer.
2. Heat a little oil or fat, then cook chopped onion until golden brown.
3. Add flour, stock, mashed potatoes and seasoning, then stir. Remove from the heat.
4. Beat the egg and add half only to the mixture. Add meat to the mixture and mix well.
5. Shape mixture into balls using a little extra flour to prevent it sticking.
6. Coat balls with remaining half of beaten egg and coat with breadcrumbs.
7. Fry in deep hot fat until golden brown.

   Drain and serve hot.

MINCE AU GRATIN

2 servings

Ingredients

Cold cooked meat—enough for 2 people
2 spoonfuls butter
4 spoonfuls gravy or sauce
6 spoonfuls grated cheese
6 spoonfuls breadcrumbs
Salt and pepper to taste

Method
1. Cut meat and pass pieces through a mincer.
2. Mix together the breadcrumbs and grated cheese.

3. Grease a casserole and put in a layer of breadcrumbs and grated cheese, then a layer of meat plus seasoning and a few spoonfuls of gravy or sauce. Repeat the layers until the dish is full.
4. Sprinkle top with rest of grated cheese and breadcrumbs.
5. Put a few pats of butter on top and bake in hot oven until nicely brown—for about 20 minutes.
Serve at once.

Variation
Cooked meat could be cut into cubes, not minced.

MINCE ROLL

2 servings

Ingredients

1 cup cooked minced meat	1 cupful breadcrumbs
2 eggs	A little chopped parsley
1 slice bacon	A little mixed herbs
1 medium sized chopped onion	Salt and pepper to taste

Method
1. Dip a clean cloth into hot water, squeeze out water, lay flat and sprinkle on some flour.
2. Mix all ingredients together.
3. Wrap the mixture in the cloth and put it into boiling water in a pan.
4. Boil in cloth for about 1½ hours.
Serve with meat gravy.

Variation
Mashed potatoes could be used instead of breadcrumbs.

MEAT CAKES

2 servings

Ingredients

1 cupful cooked minced meat	1 spoonful margarine
1 cupful cooked mashed potatoes	A little breadcrumbs or flour
1 egg	A little oil or fat
	Salt and pepper to taste

Method
1. Melt margarine and mix into it meat and potatoes, then cool.
2. Add some of beaten egg and seasoning.
3. Form into cake sizes coating with breadcrumbs or the flour.
4. Coat cakes with remaining egg and fry in hot fat or oil for about 10 minutes until inside is well cooked.
5. Drain well and serve hot.

Variation
Use fish instead of mince meat but make sure all bones have been removed first.

ONION HASH

2 servings

Ingredients

1 cupful, or 4 spoonfuls, minced meat or chopped cooked meat	2 spoonfuls butter or margarine
2 medium sized chopped onions	Salt and pepper to taste

Method
1. Brown onions in margarine and add meat.
2. Cook for 3 minutes, seasoning well.
3. Serve hot with mashed potatoes.

FISH PIE

2 servings

Ingredients

Cooked fish—enough for 2 people	1 spoonful margarine
2 small sized potatoes	2 spoonfuls flour
1 hard-boiled egg	1½ cupfuls milk
	Salt and pepper to taste

Method

1. Peel, wash and cook potatoes, then mash with a little of the milk.
2. Melt margarine in a saucepan, add flour, stir and then add rest of milk to form a sauce.
3. Cook slowly for about 10 minutes until ready.
4. Remove bones and skin from the fish, flake it and add it to the sauce. Add the chopped egg, then seasoning.
5. Put mixture into greased pie-dish, cover with potatoes and bake in moderate oven for about 30 minutes until nicely browned.

Serve hot.

PUDDINGS

FRUIT SALAD AND CHOPPED GROUNDNUTS

4 servings

Ingredients

Mixed fruits—enough for 4 people
1 cupful fruit juice
1 spoonful sugar
2 spoonfuls groundnuts

Method
1. Peel all the fruit and remove seeds. Cut into neat cubes and put into dish.
2. Fry groundnuts, chop them up and add to fruit.
3. Boil fruit juice with sugar, strain and pour over fruit. Allow to cool.
4. Decorate top of pudding with pieces of banana or cherries. Serve with cream or custard.

N.B. Fruits suitable for this salad are: grenadilla, paw paw, pineapple, mangoes, oranges, bananas, apples and pears.
Fruits which produce juice are, grenadilla, pineapple, lemons, oranges, tangerines, grapefruit and guavas.

JELLY

6 servings

Ingredients
1 packet jelly crystals   2 cupfuls water

Method
1. Heat water to boiling point. Empty packet of jelly crystals into an enamel or glass jug.
2. Pour hot water over jelly and stir constantly until jelly is dissolved.
3. Pour into a glass dish and leave in a cool place until jelly is completely set.
Serve with cream or custard.

N.B.   Sometimes jelly in packet is solid. If so cut it with scissors into smallish pieces.

Variations
(a) For jelly cream, add 1 cupful of cream just before jelly is set. Stir in well and pour into a mould.
(b) For jellied fruit, add some neatly cubed mixed fruits into jelly just before it is set but do not use raw pineapple.
(c) For jellied sponge fill mould with small pieces of sponge cake and pour jelly over it.

BAKED CUSTARD

2 servings

Ingredients
1½ cupfuls milk   2 spoonfuls sugar
2 eggs   A little flavouring, such as vanilla

Method
1. Heat the milk to boiling point and beat the eggs well.
2. Add milk into eggs little by little and mix well.
3. Add sugar and flavouring and strain into a small greased pie-dish.
4. Stand the dish in a little water in a roasting pan.
5. Bake in a slow oven for about ½ hour.

GRENADILLA SPONGE

6 servings

Ingredients

12 grenadillas	3 spoonfuls sugar
1 cupful water	Juice from 2 medium sized oranges
2 eggs	2 spoonfuls gelatine

Method
1. Scrape out fruit from grenadillas and cook in the water.
2. Press grenadilla juice through a sieve and add orange juice, sugar and gelatine previously soaked in a little cold water.
3. Put all into a saucepan and heat until gelatine is dissolved.
4. Beat in the egg yolks and continue to beat until mixture has cooled.
5. Beat well egg whites and add to the mixture just when it begins to set.
6. Pour into a mould and allow to set completely.
7. Turn out on to a dish and serve with cream or custard.

Variation
Any other fruits such as lemons, oranges, paw-paw or pineapple could be used, but do not cook them in water.

BANANA FRITTERS

2 servings

Ingredients

2 ripe bananas	4 teaspoonfuls milk
2 egg whites	2 spoonfuls flour
1 spoonful sugar	2 spoonfuls salad oil

Method
1. Mix flour, sugar, milk and egg in a bowl. Mix well and leave for ½ hour.
2. Heat salad oil in a frying pan.
3. Peel and split bananas lengthwise, dip each into mixture and fry in hot fat.

Serve hot.

Variation
   Other fruits such as pineapple and apples, could be used instead of bananas.

FRUIT FOOL

Fruits which can be used for this dish:
Bananas—mash ripe bananas, add sugar and a little lemon juice.
Apple—Peel, cut up into pieces and bake or boil until soft. Add sugar and a few cloves.
Pineapple—mince it, catching juice in a bowl. Add sugar to taste. Cook until tender.
Mangoes—peel, cut flesh into small pieces, steam and add sugar when nearly ready. Put through a coarse sieve.
Guava—peel, cut in halves and stew in a little water until tender. Put through a coarse sieve. Add sugar to taste.
Grenadilla—scoop out seeds, add very little water and sugar to taste. Boil a little then strain.

6 servings

Ingredients
Fruit—enough for 6 people—any one mentioned above
2 egg whites
8 spoonfuls sugar
A little flavouring
A little water

Method
1. Prepare fruit chosen as above and cook according to instructions.
2. Put in a serving dish.
3. Whip stiffly whites of eggs, add flavouring and a little food colouring if desired. Place on top of fruit.

   Serve very cold with whipped cream or custard.

BOILED CUSTARD

2 servings

Ingredients
2 cupfuls milk   Sugar to taste
2 eggs   Flavouring if desired

Method
1. Boil milk with sugar and allow it to cool a little.
2. Beat up eggs and add it to milk stirring constantly.
3. Place in a jug in saucepan of boiling water and stir until it thickens.
4. Serve as a sauce to go with fruit salad or other pudding or serve by itself.

Variation
   Mix 2 spoonfuls of cornflour with a little cold milk and add to custard mixture.

GROUND RICE PUDDING

2 servings

Ingredients
2 spoonfuls ground rice   1 egg
2 spoonfuls sugar   A pinch salt
3 cupfuls milk   Flavouring as desired

Method
1. Bring milk to the boil and stir in ground rice until milk is boiling. Boil gently for 5 minutes and then cool.
2. Add sugar and well beaten egg and pinch of salt and then mix thoroughly.
3. Pour into a greased pie-dish and bake in moderately hot oven until nicely browned—about 20 minutes.

   Serve hot or cold.

Variations
   (a) The yolk of the egg could be added first, after which the stiffly beaten white added to make a very light pudding.
   (b) Other grains, such as semolina, cornflour, maize-flour, etc. could be used instead of ground rice.

RICE AND APPLE PUDDING

4 servings

Ingredients

2 large sized apples	3 cupfuls milk
2 spoonfuls rice	A pinch salt
13 spoonfuls sugar	A little water
2 eggs	

Method
1. Clean rice, add milk and cook slowly in a pan until rice is soft.
2. Peel, core and quarter apples and then stew with only 4 spoonfuls of the sugar and a little water.
3. Separate the eggs and beat the yolks. Add this to the rice together with only one spoon of sugar and a pinch of salt.
4. Pour into a greased pie-dish and arrange the apples on top.
5. Whisk the egg whites stiffly, add only 7 spoonfuls of sugar and place on top of the mixture.
6. Sprinkle with remaining 1 spoonful of sugar and bake in moderately hot oven for ½ hour.

Serve hot or cold with cream or any other sauce.

Variations
(a) Other fruit such as pineapples or mangoes could be used instead of apple.
(b) Other grains such as semolina or sago could be used instead of rice.

RICE PUDDING

2 servings

Ingredients

2 spoonfuls whole rice
2 spoonfuls sugar
3 cupfuls milk
1 teaspoonful butter or margarine
Flavouring as desired.

Method
1. Wash rice thoroughly.
2. Mix all ingredients and put into a greased pie-dish.
3. Bake in a moderately hot oven, stirring frequently for about 30 minutes until creamy and nicely browned on top.

   Serve hot or cold.

Variation

Fruit, such as apples or pineapples, could be chopped and added before cooking.

GENERAL

EGGS

Use only fresh eggs when preparing dishes from eggs. A fresh egg is heavy, clear when looked through in a strong light and it will sink when put into water.

Egg dishes are usually served for breakfast and supper. In most African homes, breakfast is very simple. Usually it consists of gruel or porridge into which milk and sugar is added, or, bread and butter taken with tea or coffee. In a home where eggs are not usually eaten for breakfast or supper, they could be served as one of the main meals to the children or invalids of the house, if the dish is prepared carefully.

Eggs are one of the cheapest ways of supplying the body with protein.

BOILED EGG—SOFT

1-2 eggs per person or more if required

Method

Place the egg in boiling water in a pan and boil for $3\frac{1}{2}$ minutes. OR—place the egg in cold water in a pan, bring to the boil and boil for 2 minutes.

BOILED EGG—HARD

1-2 eggs per person or more if required

Method
    Place the egg in cold water, bring to the boil and boil for 12 minutes.

N.B. Boiled eggs are usually served with buttered toast or bread.

ONION OMELETTE

servings

Ingredients
2 eggs
1 small sized onion
2 spoonfuls oil or ghee
Salt and pepper to taste

Method
1. Chop the onions finely.
2. Heat the ghee or oil until smoking hot.
3. Beat eggs in a bowl and add onions and seasoning.
4. Pour in egg mixture, into oil, and cook until brown. Turn to other side and cook until ready.

Serve at once and eat immediately with toasted bread or chipped potatoes.

Variations
(a) Any other chopped food such as cooked mushroom, tomatoes, ham, cheese, liver, even cooked fish could be used to vary the dish.
(b) Onions could be fried first before adding to the eggs.

POACHED EGG

1 serving

Ingredients
1-2 eggs per person or more as required
1 slice buttered toast
½ cupful water
1 teaspoon lime juice
Salt to taste

Method
1. Boil water in a flat pan and add salt and lime juice. The lime juice helps to set the egg.
2. Break the egg into a cup and slip it gently into the boiling water.
3. Cook for 2½ minutes basting with hot water all the time.
4. Lift from water using a fish slice and place on hot buttered toast.

Serve hot.

FRIED EGG

2 servings

Ingredients
1-2 eggs per person or more if required
2 spoonfuls fat or oil

Method
1. Heat fat in a frying pan.
2. Break the eggs carefully into a cup and place gently into the pan. Do not break the yolk. Keep as small as possible and baste all the time with hot fat until lightly set.
3. Remove from pan and serve hot.

N.B. Fried eggs can be served together with toast, fried bacon, cooked beans, fried sausages, liver or kidney.

SCRAMBLED EGG

2 servings

Ingredients
2 eggs
4 spoonfuls milk
1 spoonful butter
2 slices toast
Salt and pepper to taste

Method
1. Melt butter in a pan and beat eggs with milk lightly, then add salt and pepper.
2. Pour egg mixture in pan and stir briskly over a low heat until it thickens and becomes creamy.
3. Pile on hot toast and serve at once.

Variation
Chopped foods such as cheese, ham, liver, sausages, kidneys, groundnuts and onions, etc. maybe added to vary this dish.

BREAD

BREAD—USUAL METHOD

6 servings

First Step:

Ingredients
7 cupfuls plain flour
1 spoonful dried yeast
½ spoonful sugar
1½ cupfuls warm water

Method
1. Place water into a mixing bowl, add yeast and sugar. Melt for 5 minutes.
2. Add flour and mix until it turns into sponge.
3. Cover with a damp cloth and leave in a warm place to swell for about 1½ hours.

Second Step:

Ingredients
3½ cupfuls Plain flour
1 spoonful margarine
½ spoonful sugar
¾ cupful water
½ spoonful salt

Method
1. Rub margarine into flour. Dissolve sugar and salt in water and mix with the sponge mixture.
2. Add mixture of flour and margarine to the sponge and mix whole into a smooth dough.
3. Cover dough in the bowl with a damp cloth and return to a warm place. Leave for 45 minutes.

Third Step:

Ingredients
1 egg   A little milk

Method
1. Divide the dough into 4 equal parts. Roll the pieces into balls and leave on table covered with a damp cloth for 10 minutes.
2. Shape the pieces to fit baking tins and knead thoroughly with the fingers and palm of hand.
3. Place dough in baking tins, cover with damp cloth and return to warm place to swell until they double their size—about 50 minutes.
4. Brush top of bread lightly with a mixture of egg and milk.
5. Bake in a hot oven until ready, about 30 minutes.

BREAD—QUICK METHOD

6 servings

Ingredients
4 cupfuls flour
2 teaspoonfuls dried yeast
1½ cupfuls water
8 spoonfuls warm water
1 teaspoonful sugar
2 teaspoonfuls salt

Method
1. Mix yeast with sugar and add 8 spoonfuls of warmed water.

2. Sieve flour into a warm bowl and add salt.
3. Make a well in centre of flour and into it pour the creamed yeast and the 1½ cupfuls of warm water.
4. Mix with a wooden spoon until it forms into a ball. Beat thoroughly and turn out on to a floured board and knead well.
5. Grease 2 bread tins and divide the dough into two equal sized portions.
6. Put one piece of dough into each tin and cover with a cloth.
7. Place tins in warm place until the dough has risen to top of tins.
8. Bake in a hot oven—gas mark 5—for 40 minutes.
9. Remove and tap sharply the bottoms of the loaves to test for readiness. If ready they will sound quite hollow.
10. Cool on a wire tray.

SCONES

12 servings

Ingredients
4 cupfuls plain flour
2 teaspoonfuls baking powder
2 eggs
2 spoonfuls margarine

A little milk
Salt and sugar to taste
1 egg or a little milk—for oven scones

Method for Making
1. Mix all dry ingredients above in a bowl plus the margarine.
2. Make a well in centre of the mixture, add eggs to the centre and mix well, then add milk.
3. Mix well and knead lightly on a floured board to prevent mixture from sticking.
4. Roll out to about ½ inch thick and cut into any desired shapes.

Method for Cooking

(a) **Oven Scones**
Place on a greased tin and brush with egg or milk. Bake in a quick oven for about 10 minutes until ready.

(b) **Girdle Scones**
Heat a hot-plate on an electric stove or heat a flat frying pan on a gas stove. Place shaped scones so that they cook gently for about 10 minutes until brown on under sides. Turn and cook on other side. Remove and cool, covered with a damp cloth.

(c) **Drop Scones**
Add more liquid—milk into the mixture until it can be dropped with a spoon when poured. Drop the mixture on a clean hot greased girdle. When the surface rises in bubbles, the underside is ready. Turn and cook other side until brown. Remove and cool in a cloth.

CAKES

CAKE MAKING

Foundation Ingredients

2 spoonfuls margarine or butter	1 teaspoonful baking powder
1 cupful sugar	½ cupful milk
1¼ cupfuls plain flour	2 eggs
	A pinch salt

Method
1. Cream margarine and sugar in a bowl, beating hard for about 10 minutes.
2. Whip eggs and stir into the mixture a little at a time. Stir well until eggs are all mixed in.
3. Mix flour, baking powder and salt and then sieve twice. Add flour to the mixture and stir lightly.
4. Add milk and beat vigorously.

VANILLA LOAF

6 servings

Ingredients

Foundation mixture (as above)

Method
1. Add one teaspoonful of vanilla essence and beat vigorously.
2. Grease a bread tin holding ½ Kg. lined with greaseproof paper. Pour the mixture into the tin and bake in a moderately hot oven for about 1 hour until ready.
3. Remove from oven and cool on a wire tray.

Serve with tea

OTHER RECIPES USING THE FOUNDATION MIXTURE

Orange Cake

Add grated peel of half an orange to the Foundation mixture and stir well. Bake in a large shallow tin in a hot oven until ready—about 20 minutes. Remove from oven and place on wire tray to cool. Cut cake into squares when serving.

Fruit Cake

Add a cupful of cleaned and chopped sultanas and raisins into the Foundation mixture and stir well. Bake in a greased cake tin lined with greaseproof paper. Cook for about 1 hour in a moderately hot oven. Cool on a wire tray.

Loaf Cake

Add a cup of figs or dates to the Foundation mixture and stir well. Bake the same way as for Vanilla Loaf Recipe.

Nut Cake

Add a cup of roasted groundnuts to the above Foundation mixture and stir well. Bake in the same way as for Fruit Cake.

Gingerbread

Instead of milk in the Foundation mixture, use syrup and instead of baking powder use bicarbonate of soda dissolved in a little milk. Add a teaspoonful of ground ginger to the mixture. Bake in the same way as for Fruit Cake.

SMALL LEMON CAKES

6 servings

Ingredients

2 spoonfuls margarine or butter
1 cupful sugar
1½ cupfuls plain flour
1 teaspoonful baking powder
½ cupful milk
2 eggs
Peel of ½ lemon
A little powdered ginger
A pinch salt

Method
1. Cream margarine and sugar in a bowl, beating hard for about 10 minutes.
2. Whip eggs and stir into the mixture a little at a time.
3. Stir well until eggs are all mixed in.
4. Mix flour, baking powder and salt and then sieve twice. Add flour to the mixture and stir lightly.
5. Add milk and beat vigorously.
6. Add grated lemon peel and a little powdered ginger. Stir well.
7. Grease small tins and place mixture in them and then sprinkle with sugar.
8. Bake in a hot oven for about 15 minutes until ready.
9. Remove from oven and cool on a wire tray.

CHOCOLATE CAKES

6 servings

Ingredients

2 spoonfuls margarine or butter
1 cupful sugar
1½ cupfuls plain flour
1 teaspoonful baking powder
½ cupful milk
2 eggs
A pinch salt
3 spoonfuls chocolate powder

Method
1. Cream margarine and sugar in a bowl, beating hard for about 10 minutes. Add into the mixture well beaten eggs a little at a time.
2. Stir well until eggs are all mixed in.
3. Mix well the flour, baking powder and salt and then sieve twice. Add flour to the mixture and stir lightly.
4. Add milk and beat vigorously.
5. Add chocolate powder and stir well.
6. Grease two tins of the same size lined with greaseproof paper.
7. Place the mixture in them and bake in a fairly hot oven for about 45 minutes until ready.
8. Remove from oven and cool in a wire tray.

BISCUITS

SHORTBREAD BISCUITS

12 servings

Ingredients

1 cupful butter
3½ cupfuls flour
4 spoonfuls castor sugar

Method
1. Place butter in a bowl and beat until soft.
2. Add sugar and beat vigorously.
3. Add flour slowly and knead mixture.
4. Press into shallow tins and prick with a fork.
5. Bake in a slow oven for about 20 minutes until ready.
6. Cool slightly and cut into shapes.

Variations
(a) Instead of castor sugar, use icing sugar or even ordinary sugar.
(b) Use 2 cupfuls flour and 1½ cupfuls rice flour instead of the ordinary flour.
(c) The yolk of one egg and 2 spoonfuls of cream could be added to the mixture.

COOKIES—AMERICAN BISCUITS

12 servings

Ingredients

4 cupfuls flour
1½ cupfuls sugar
½ cupful milk

8 spoonfuls margarine
¼ teaspoonful salt
½ teaspoonful bicarbonate of soda

Method
1. Put margarine, sugar, milk and bicarbonate of soda in a saucepan and bring to boil.
2. Allow to cool and then mix with flour.
3. Knead well, roll out and cut into squares or rounds. Prick well with a fork and put in a slow oven for about 20 minutes until ready.
4. Cool on a wire tray and keep in an airtight tin.

DISHES FOR INVALIDS

GRUEL

Ingredients
2 spoonfuls finger millet flour
3 cupfuls water
1 cupful boiled milk
Sugar to taste

Method
1. Place flour in a lined pan and cover with water and leave to soak for 30 minutes.
2. Bring to the boil stirring constantly then simmer for 15 minutes.
3. Serve hot and then add milk and sugar to taste.

Variation
Any type of flour or even oatmeal could be used. Oatmeal should be soaked for 1 hour and then strained.

BEEF TEA

2 servings

Ingredients
Lean and juicy beef—enough for two
3 cupfuls cold water
Salt to taste

Method
1. Wipe meat thoroughly and remove all fat.
2. Scrape and place in a clean glass jar together with water and salt.
3. Cover glass jar and leave to stand for ½ hour, pressing the meat from time to time.
4. Cover the top of glass jar with greaseproof paper then stand it in cold water in a pan and bring to the boil.
5. Simmer slowly for 2-3 hours on a very gentle heat.
6. Skim surface to remove all grease and fat.
7. Strain and serve hot.

Variation—Quick method

Prepare as above but soak only for a few minutes. Place in a pan and stir gently until just boiling and simmer for 10-15 minutes. Finish as above.

BEEF TEA CUSTARD

2 servings

Ingredients
2 cupfuls beef tea   A pinch salt
2 egg yolks

Method
1. Beat the eggs and add beef tea and salt, and beat well until thoroughly mixed.
2. Strain into a buttered dish and cover with greaseproof paper.
3. Boil water in another pan, then place custard dish into boiling water and reduce heat.
4. Cook for 20 minutes until firm.

Serve hot or cold.

LEMONADE

2 servings

Ingredients
2 lemons   2 spoonfuls sugar
2 cupfuls boiling water

Method
1. Wipe the lemon then remove the skin.
2. Place the skin in a clean bowl and add boiling water.
3. Allow to stand for 10 minutes, covered and add juice from the lemons and sugar.
4. Strain and when cold, serve.

EGG FLIP

1 serving

Ingredients
1 egg   1 teaspoonful sugar
½ cupful milk

Method
1. Beat egg—which must be fresh—then add sugar.
2. Put in a tumbler and then heat the milk.
3. Add milk gradually into the egg and stir well.

   Serve hot.
N.B. A teaspoonful of brandy could be added if required.

RICE WATER

2 servings

Ingredients
2 spoonfuls rice   5 cupfuls water

Method
1. Wash rice carefully in cold water.
2. Soak in tepid water and leave on top of warm stove for 3 hours.
3. Boil slowly for 1 hour then strain.

4. Leave to cool, then serve, adding any flavouring which the invalid is allowed.

N.B. This drink is useful in cases of diarrhoea or dysentery.

CHICKEN SOUP

2 servings

1 boiler chicken
5 cupfuls water
1 spoonful rice

1 medium sized onion
Salt to taste

Method
1. Clean chicken and cut into big pieces.
2. Place in a clean pan and cover with water. Bring slowly to boiling point and then simmer for 3 hours.
3. Strain and add rice which has been cleaned well.
4. Boil for 15 minutes until rice is cooked then add chopped onion or some parsley.

Serve hot.

LIVER SOUP

2 servings
Ingredients
Enough liver for 2
5 cupfuls water

1 medium sized onion
Salt and pepper to taste

Method
1. Wash liver in salted water and cut it up into small pieces.
2. Cover with water in a clean saucepan and add chopped onions and seasoning.
3. Allow to simmer very gently for ¾ hour.
4. Remove from heat and rub through a fine clean sieve.
5. Heat again and serve hot.

Part 3

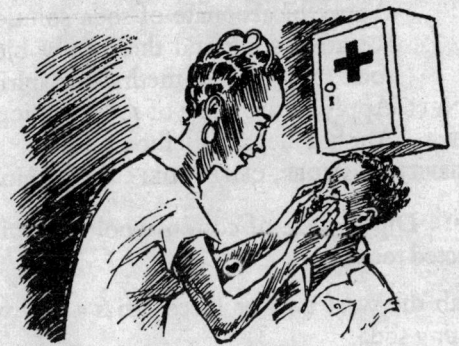

HOME REMEDIES AND HOUSEHOLD HINTS

Bruises: Finger or foot shut in a door, etc. Put the affected part alternately in very hot water then in very cold water.

Burns: Apply linen cloth soaked in bicarbonate of soda mixed with water.

Fishbone in Throat: A large piece of *ugali* or fresh bread should be swallowed in one piece. If this fails, give something to make the person vomit, e.g. salty water. If this fails, make the person suck the juice from a lemon.

Nairobi Eye: This is a bite from a Nairobi Fly. Apply immediately milk or calamine lotion or bicarbonate of soda mixed with water.

Prickly Heat: Apply a thick paste of milk and bicarbonate of soda at night and dust with talcum powder or calamine lotion through the day.

Ringworm: Paint the spot with iodine or with ordinary writing ink daily until ringworm disappears.

Scalds: Spread dry bicarbonate of soda over scald immediately and cover quickly with a cloth leaving the cloth on the affected part until heat is entirely extracted. Or, immerse the affected part in a solution of bicarbonate of soda and water (one teaspoonful to 3 cups).

Sore Lips: Apply mixture of equal parts of lemon juice and glycerine with a small piece of cotton wool.

Sting: ANT: Apply bicarbonate of soda solution, or, soda.
BEE: Remove sting and then apply bicarbonate of soda solution, or, methylated spirit.
HORNET: Apply bicarbonate of soda solution.
WASP: Apply vinegar or lemon juice.
CATERPILLAR, SPIDER, CENTIPEDE: As for Hornet.

Tooth-ache: Dip a piece of cotton wool in a spirit and push on to the affected tooth.

Warts: Rub the wart two or three times a day with a damp piece of washing soda.

Mouth-Wash: During an illness when the breath might smell, add 2 teaspoonfuls of lemon juice, or, ½ teaspoonful of bicarbonate of soda, to a tumbler of water.

POISONS

Give something immediately which will cause vomiting. Such a thing is called an emetic which counteracts the poison inside a person.

Alcohol: Give black coffee.

Rat Poison: Give an emetic and when it has acted, give the person plenty of lime water, raw egg and milk, followed by large doses of castor oil.

Iodine: Give an emetic and when this has acted, give the person starch water, boiled potatoes in milk or egg and milk drinks.

Toadstools or False Mushrooms: Give an emetic and when it has acted give the person whisky or brandy. In severe cases apply friction to the stomach and place a mustard plaster over it.

Unknown Poisons: Give the person plenty of lukewarm water or milk immediately followed by two raw eggs. If the person collapses, give strong black coffee, black tea, brandy or whisky.

HOUSEHOLD HINTS

Aluminium Cooking Utensils: To clean, rub with fine soapy steel wool. Never use soda water nor washing soda.

Blood Stains: To remove from clothes, soak for 1 hour in lukewarm water to which a little salt has been added, then wash with soap.

Boots and Shoes: To soften after a long period in which they have not been worn, wash well in warm water and then rub in castor oil or any other oil.

Burning Oil: To extinguish, throw on sand, earth or salt. Never throw on water as it will only cause the fire to spread.

Burnt Saucepans: Fill with salt and water and leave until the following day. Heat to boiling point then wash with a rag.

Clothing on fire: Wrap a blanket tightly round the person and heat the affected place, or, wrap the person in a blanket and make him roll over and over on the floor.

Drawers and Cupboard Doors: To prevent from sticking, rub a bar of hard soap over the lower edges, then polish it.

Feet: For tired feet, soak them in hot salty water and then rub them with boracic powder mixed with dry starch.

Finger Marks: To remove from painted doors or window-frames, apply a few drops of paraffin to a flannel or soft rag and rub lightly.

Fleas: To get rid of fleas from bedrooms, remove all bedclothes and take them outside into the sun and air. Sprinkle them with insect powder. Allow plenty of air and light into the bedroom.

Flowers: Revive flowers in vases by cutting off small pieces of the stems every day. Add a little salt and soda to the water.

Picking Maize off the Cob: Remove a few grains at a time, using a strong kitchen knife and following one row from top to bottom of the cob. When one row is done, leave the knife and remove the grains by hand, one row at a time till all the grains are removed.

Blocked Pipes: Force a mixture of washing soda and salt as far as possible down the drain or pipe. Pour boiling water through the pipe ½ hour later.

Soap: To economise with soap, small old pieces should be chopped or shredded thinly and then put into an empty tin with very little cold water and heated until the soap dissolves. The soap jelly can then be used in the kitchen.

Tea: To economise use of tea, crush the tea-leaves on a board and use less measures. Do not crush to a dust.

INDEX

Avocado pears,
  with hard boiled egg, 94
  with chopped prawns, 95
  with oil and vinegar, 95
  with fish, 95
  with chicken, 96

Bacon and egg, fried, 105
Barbecue,
  pork chop, 103
  shish kebab, 87
Beef,
  roast, 99
  boiled and carrots, 114
Biscuits,
  groundnut, 35
  savoury cassava, 59
  shortbread, 141
Bread,
  brown maize meal, 40
  groundnut, 34
  sweet potato, 54
  usual method, 135
  quick method, 136

Cakes,
  maize meal, 45
  maize meal sandwich, 46
  maize meal rock, 48
  sweet potato, 53
  meat, 123
  chocolate, 140
Cassava,
  baked and sweet corn, 57
  cheese balls in batter, 57
  cheese pie of, 58
  cakes, 59
  scones of, 60
Chapati, 91
Chicken,
  stew, 26
  stewed in groundnut sauce, 26
  roast boned, 27
  green maize and minced, 44
  roast, 100
  fried in breadcrumbs, 104
  stewed, 111
  boiled, 114
  mushroom and rice casserole, 101
  pilau 88,
  tandoori, 86
Cheese, sweet potato and onion casserole, 56
Chips, sweet potato, 53
Chops and Liver, fried, 106
Coconut,
  milk, 66
  sauce, 67-8
  salad, 68
  cones, 68
  biscuits, 69
  and sweet potato pudding, 69
Coconut Curry, and fish, 89
Cookies, American biscuits, 142
Cow blood, cookery, 81
Cow's blood,
  cooked in sour milk, 81
  cooked in cold milk, 81
Curry paste or Curry sauce, 93
Custard,
  baked, 125
  beef tea, 144
  green maize, 45

Dengu, 73

Ebinyebwa (groundnut sauce), 32
  Chicken in, see (chicken stewed in groundnut sauce)
Egg plant, stuffed, 109
Egg,
  boiled—soft, 132
  boiled—hard, 133
  poached, 133
  fried, 134
  scrambled, 134
Egg flip, 145
Eggs,
  cassava scotch, 60
  scotch, 108

Fish,
  fried, 29, 104
  stewed, 112
  grilled with orange butter, 115
  baked (A), 115
  baked (B), 116
Finger millet, flour porridge, 75
Fritters,
  maize meal, 47
  pumpkin savoury, 79

Grasshoppers or Locusts, fried, 85
Gruel, 143

Invalids, dishes for, 143
Irio, 71

Jelly, 125

"Kamongo/Monye,"
  fried fillet, of, 31
  smoked, 30
  stewed, 30

151

Index

"Kat Ayienya" (Luo), 83
Kebab, barbecue, 102

Lake fish, fried with groundnut sauce, 28
Lamb or mutton, curried, 89
Lamb pie, minced, 109
Lemon cakes, small, 140
Lemonade, 145
Loaf, vanilla, 139

Maize,
    Flour and rice, fried, 37
    green, 37
    baked and eggs, 39
    baked and tomatoes, 39
    doughnuts (mandazi), 41
    pie, 41
    pancakes, 49
    in mayonnaise, 43
    meal biscuits, 42
    meal pudding, 50
    meal sponge, 51,

Matoke,
    cooked in milk, 63
    browned, 63
    crispie, 64
    cake sandwiches with minced meat, 64
    chips, deep fried, 65
    with beans, 65, 66
    steamed with stewed chicken, 62

Meat,
    minced and onions, 111
    smoked (biltong) stewed, 22
    in coconut milk, 23
    and vegetable stew, 24
    and green maize stew, 24
    barbecue, 25
    fried balls of, 108
Mixtures, 71
Mud fish or Lung fish, see under "Kamongo/Monye".

Mushrooms,
    dried and greens, 77
    pounded, 78
Mutura and Mahu, stuffed, 82
Mutton, curried, 110
Mince au Gratin, 121

Ngege, 25
    (also see Lake fish fried with groundnut sauce)
Nyoyo, 72

Omelette,
    green maize, 44
    Onion, 133
Onion, hash 123

Pancakes, maize, 49
Pie,
    cottage or shepheard's, 120
    fish, 124
Potatoes, roast, 100
Pudding,
    sweet potatoes, in coconut milk, 52
    Coconut, 70
    Yorkshire, 118
    ground rice, 129
    rice and apple, 130
    rice, 131
    fruit salad and chopped groundnut, 125
    grenadilla sponge, 127
    banana fritters, 127
    fruit fool, 128
    boiled custard, 129

Rice,
    coconut, 66
    and bean stew, 72
Rice water, 145
Rissoles, 121
Roast, pot, 101
Rolls,
    maize meal, 48
    cassava flour, 61
    mince, 122
Roti, 90

Samosa, 92
Sauce, mayonnaise, 105
Sausages,
    and bacon, fried, 106